AIMS, INFLUENCE AND CHANGE IN THE
PRIMARY SCHOOL CURRICULUM

MONOGRAPH No. 1

AIMS, INFLUENCE AND CHANGE IN THE
PRIMARY SCHOOL CURRICULUM

Monographs in Curriculum Studies
General Editor: Philip H. Taylor
In association with:
Anne Hurman
Penelope Weston

Supported in part by an SSRC Grant

Aims, Influence and Change in the Primary School Curriculum

Edited by Professor P. H. Taylor
Head of Curriculum and Method
Division, Birmingham University
School of Education

NFER Publishing Company

Published by the NFER Publishing Company Ltd.,
Book Division, 2 Jennings Buildings, Thames Avenue,
Windsor, Berks., SL4 1QS
Registered Office, The Mere, Upton Park, Slough, Berks., SL1 2DQ
First Published 1975
© P. H. Taylor 1975
85633 072 8

Printed in Great Britain by
John Sherratt & Son Ltd.,
The St Anne's Press,
Park Road, Altrincham, Cheshire, WA14 5QQ

Distributed in the USA by Humanities Press Inc.,
Hillary House-Fernhill House, Atlantic Highlands,
New Jersey 07716, USA

Contents

Acknowledgements   7

Introduction   9

Part I
Aims in Primary Education   13

1. Two Analyses of Teachers' Discussions of aims in
   Primary Education   15
   Frances R. Davies and Patricia M. Ashton

2. A Study of the Emphasis given by Teachers of Different
   Age Groups to Aims in Primary Education   46
   Philip H. Taylor and Brian Holley

Part II
Curriculum Change   73

3. Primary School Teachers' Perceptions of Discovery Learning   75
   Colin Richards

4. An Exercise in Managing Curriculum Development in a
   Primary School   103
   Peter Evans and Maurice Groarke

Part III
Curricular Influences   139

5. Tradition and Change in the Primary School Curriculum in
   Northern Ireland   141
   P. T. McConnellogue

6. A Study of the Curricular Influences in a Mid-Western
   Elementary School System   170
   Philip H. Taylor

Acknowledgements

First thanks are to the contributors who all kept to the deadline, and were very patient with my editing. To them I am grateful.

Second thanks, and just as heartfelt, go to Mrs Audrey Witherford who typed the manuscript and collated it.

Finally, my thanks to my colleagues Ann Hurman and Bill Reid who made helpful comments.

Introduction

The six papers collected in this volume represent attempts to study aspects of the primary school curriculum, its aims, its development, the influences to which it is subjected and the perceptions of the teachers whose job it is to give meaning to the curriculum. They are also contributions to curriculum studies.

The primary school curriculum can be studied either as *what it is intended should be taught*, i.e. the purposes to be served, the aims and objectives to be pursued, subject matter to be taught (and how these may change); or as *what is taught*, i.e., the skills, capabilities and attitudes which teachers actually seek to develop. This is not a new enterprise. Since primary schools began, their curricula have been the object of interest. What is perhaps new is the objectivity of many of the studies now being undertaken. They present ordered, systematic data in supporting the claims which they make about the nature of the curriculum of the primary school; data which exist in their own right, independently of the observer, and which make it increasingly possible to construct a picture of the primary school curriculum in all its complexity.

Curriculum Studies

To someone new to curriculum studies the way in which the term curriculum has been interpreted in this collection of papers may seem somewhat broad. The conventional meaning of curriculum as *a course of study* conveys a picture of something static, laid out, fixed and given, and in a sense this is how *a* curriculum may be seen. In this case, the only job to be done in studying it is to describe its content. However, if we ask, What were the origins of the curriculum? How was it developed? and What purpose was it intended to serve? it becomes evident that studies which answer such questions will need to look at change and the reasons for it, the justifications people give, and how they go about making their valuations. It is the dynamics of curriculum development and the ways in which those involved in it act that will be the object of study. And not only will the way they act be a fit subject for study, but also the perceptions which inform these actions.

Not only is a curriculum developed, it is also enacted, given meaning

9

and substance, through teaching. How this takes place is also an object of study. What processes are involved? How do they function and with what effect? Such questions become important. It is here, in studying the curriculum in operation, that the perceptions of those involved become of interest; perceptions tend to govern actions and judgements, and teachers, giving meaning to the curriculum, depend on both.

One other point needs to be made before the relevance of the six studies of this volume is discussed. Curricula are found in institutional settings in schools, colleges and universities, where it is necessary to provide the means which will enable the teaching and learning which the curricula call for to take place. Institutions are set in a wider social environment with which they enter into relationships and from which they are influenced. The institutional settings in which curricula are to be found and may be influenced and constrained, are of considerable importance for understanding why curricula are what they are, and in explaining their resistance (or readiness) to change.

The Studies
The studies are presented in three parts. The first focuses on the aims of primary education, the purposes which govern the curriculum for young children. Davies and Ashton present an analysis of how teachers discuss two of the major aims of primary education. They show what criteria teachers employ in their discussions and the resources of experience and information on which they draw. In many ways the study is unique. There is little dependable knowledge about how teachers formulate for themselves the meaning of the aims which they pursue. Very few attempts have been made to analyse the discourse of teachers, even of such a crucially important matter as the aims which give direction to what they teach.

Taylor and Holley take another view of aims—which aims are emphasized at different ages and phases by teachers in primary schools? They use as their data the ratings of teachers in a national sample of primary schools and subject them to several different forms of analysis. In accounting for the differences in emphasis on aims by primary school teachers they suggest that these differences serve to involve the child progressively in the educational process.

Part II, taking a broad view of curriculum change, offers studies of how teachers see the concept of *discovery learning*; a concept which has played an important part in the curriculum changes which have taken place in the last ten years in primary education, and of the problems in redeveloping the language curriculum in a small primary school. Both studies illustrate some of the complexities, perceptual and personal, which curriculum development may involve.

Both the studies in Part III examine the primary school curriculum in a non-English setting, thereby providing scope for comparison, in terms of the influences and constraints to which it is subjected.

P. H. Taylor

The University,
Birmingham

PART I

AIMS IN PRIMARY EDUCATION

Two Analyses of Teachers' Discussions of Aims in Primary Education*

F. R. Davies (University of Birmingham)
P. M. E. Ashton (University of Leicester)

Introduction

Descriptions of teachers' discussions are rare and consequently there exists almost no record of how teachers discuss educational topics. In the early stages of the Aims of Primary Education Project several teachers' discussion groups were formed to consider the aims of primary education. Full details of the composition of these discussion groups is given elsewhere (Ashton et al., 1974). The seven discussion groups composed of all grades of teachers from heads to probationers. The group meetings were arranged at schools, colleges of education and the University. Teachers who volunteered to take part in the discussions were invited to choose a convenient group.

Fourteen group leaders were chosen and each pair was asked to be responsible for a discussion group. The leaders and their functions have been described in detail (op. cit). They included college of education lecturers, teachers and inspectors. The main function of the leaders was to record the discussions and liaise with the Project team. Leaders were requested to be very informal in their conduct of meetings. They announced the topic and only interjected sufficiently to maintain the flow of discussion.

The recordings of the discussions were transcribed by typists on the Project team. The analysis of the discussion groups described in this paper was based on the typed transcripts; each discussion was analysed from two points of view.

* This study was carried out under a grant from the Schools Council for a study of the Aims of Primary Education.

The first analysis was concerned with the style of the discussion Are 'aims' discussions practical and closely related to classroom experience or are they academic and closely related, say, to educational research and theory? Are statements about aims considered to be personal opinions, given and accepted as beliefs and not questioned or analysed as to their empirical base or logical structure? One analysis presented in this study attempts to describe the style of the discussion from this point of view.

The second analysis studied the number of sub-topics or themes which were discussed under the general heading of 'aims'. One of the interests of this analysis is the width of the discussion as evidenced by the number of sub-themes discussed. This analysis also shows which themes were considered relevant to the discussions of aims: whether aims were considered from a purely academic point of view or whether other influences were taken into account, such influences as the social needs of the child, parental wishes or some theoretical model of psychological development. Also shown is the relative number of pure definitions of aims compared with a consideration of the balance between aims or of the optimum order in which to pursue them. Subsidiary issues dealt with in the analysis include the proportion of the discussion devoted to procedure and to defining educational terms. An examination of the way in which themes change over the duration of the discussion was made and the results are presented in the study.

Although this study was concerned with how teachers discuss aims, some points of wider interest emerge. Consideration of these may lead to a more sophisticated approach to the discussion of broad educational topics, and may be of practical value to teachers.

Background

The first and second stages of the Aims of Primary Education Project were designed to discover something of how teachers write about aims and something of how they talk about them. The purpose was to acquire information on which to base an appropriate and structured brief for later discussions.

Seventy volunteer teachers were sent a questionnaire which, after questions about their background, career-history and present post, concluded with the question, 'What in your opinion are the aims of Primary education? Please express these as a list of statements numbered 1, 2, 3, etc.'

The statements made in answer to this question were grouped on a simple basis of similarity of intention. Four major groups resulted.

These were:

(1) to develop the basic skills and to build up knowledge;
(2) to develop the child's capacity to think;
(3) to develop the full potential of the individual child in all aspects;
(4) to foster the child's moral and social development.

The 70 volunteer teachers were formed into seven groups and each group asked to hold four one-hour meetings, at each of which one of the four statements would be discussed. No prior notice was given of the discussion topic nor were any suggestions made as to the form the discussion should take. It was intended to elicit from the teachers as nearly as possible the ordinary, spontaneous comments and statements that they would make about these aims and to reveal how they would handle the discussion and what they thought relevant to it. The discussions were extremely informal, with two members acting as joint-leaders to announce the topic and maintain the flow of discussion.

This report is an analysis of all seven discussions of the first area of aims, ('to develop the basic skills and build up knowledge') and of three discussions of the fourth area ('to foster the child's moral and social development').

Introduction to the Analysis

Objectives of the analysis

A total of 11 one-hour tape recordings were analysed. Each recording was of a complete discussion session. All seven group discussions of the topic, 'to develop the basic skills and build up knowledge' were analysed, as were four of the group discussions on the topic 'to foster the child's moral and social development'. The recordings were transcribed verbatim and the analyses performed on the full transcripts.

The choice of analytic techniques

Verbatim discussions are notoriously difficult to analyse, and very little previous work appears to have been carried out with this type of material. The established content—analysis techniques are not considered entirely satisfactory for such discourse (Stone, Smith, Ogilvie, 1966).

Any approach using grammatical/linguistic techniques is extremely complex and time consuming. The few grammars which have been devised for sequences of verbal material are somewhat rudimentary and specialized in their application. Obviously the relation between meaning

B

and grammatical structure is complex,[1] and there is no clear relationship between grammatical structure and the information about aims conveyed in the statements. A grammatical analysis is, therefore, of minor value for the purposes under consideration. It was decided, therefore, to sacrifice a lengthy and detailed linguistic or content analysis for an intuitive, judging technique which is probably as satisfactory for this sort of material as any other available at the present time.

The classificatory systems

Two classificatory systems were devised to describe the discussion statements in ways which would provide the required information.

A: Model A was devised to gain an impression of the style of discussion by examining the intention of the teachers' contributions. The object of this classification was to examine the nature of the contributions to discussions about aims. Would such discussions be primarily opinion-exchanging exercises? Would evidence or justification be given for stated views? Would teachers question each other about their views? and so on. In order to obtain this information, statements were classified into opinions,[2] questions, references to classroom experiences, proposals, and so on. This classification owes much to the work of Bales (1951). Additional categories were devised to cover the particular character of the discussions. Thus the categories were extended to eight (see Table I), in order to reveal references specifically to academic sources and teaching experiences.

A full description of Model A is given in Table 1 below.

B: Model B was more complex, and classified statements according to the aspect of the discussion topic to which they referred. The main object of this classification was to examine the range of themes considered relevant to the general topic. Would teachers confine their attention to stating and defining aims, would their major interest be in relating aims to classroom practice or would the discussions range over a number of aspects of a more theoretical and philosophical nature? In other words, how narrow or how wide and diffuse might be the field

---

[1] Examples of similar grammar and different meaning— Examples of different grammar and similar meaning— 'I entirely agree with you'. 'I absolutely disagree with you'. 'We should teach the child to be systematic.' 'Yes, systematic knowledge is important.' 'You mean a basic skill of being systematic'.

[2] Examples of the different types of statement are given in Appendix 1.

covered in discussing aims ? As well as examining the range of themes, this analysis shows the amount of attention devoted to each theme, as measured by the number of statements made about each one.

The presentation of results
It is not possible to describe 'normal' discussion behaviour in any absolute sense. Each discussion so far as we know, is influenced by such factors as specific situations, the question being discussed, the personality of participants and so on. It was felt therefore that a useful approach would be to establish our own 'norm' for the discussions under consideration. This was done by pooling the results for seven discussion groups on the same topic and analysing overall totals. Differences between the separate discussions and the pooled results were not large enough to reach statistical significance. It was, therefore, felt safe to assume that the groups were sufficiently homogeneous to be treated together.

The Analysis by Model A
Precis I method
Verbatim discussions are not simple to analyse. Speech is multipurpose. Besides conveying meanings, ideas and facts about the topic discussed, it conveys signals concerning inter-personal relations, helps or hinders the flow of discussions and comments on the discussion or the participants. As well as this multipurpose quality, speech is complex in grammatical structure, repetitive, and includes a large amount of irrelevant 'noise'.

We are all familiar with the 'ums' and 'ers' that give the speaker time to collect his thoughts. Many of the longer 'time fillers' appear extremely strange when read, because we are used to such material being pre-edited for written material. When listening to speech we are so used to such language that it presents no difficulty. Example 1 gives an idea of the complexity and repetitiveness of speech.[1]

Example 1

'As Mr X has so well expressed this but I would like to give emphasis to the acquisition of basic skills which are fundamental and absolutely necessary, yes um, they are fundamental and absolutely necessary as every teacher does realize to the whole fabric of education and not as one particular thing.'

[1] An example of a sequence of the original speech is given in Appendix 2.

For the purpose of this study non-required material was edited out and only the sections containing information about aims were retained.

Example 1A: The precised version of Example 1 (Precis I)

'The acquisition of Basic Skills is fundamental and necessary and must be seen within the whole fabric of education.'

As will be seen this precis reduced the speech by deleting surplus material. For Precis 1 no change in order was made and the original wording was retained. Precis 1 statements were used in the analysis by Model A.

The detailed description of Model A is given in Table 1 below:

Table 1: Model A

	Symbol	Category Title	Description
(1)	O+	OPINION : GIVING	Covers all statements of opinion.
(2)	O−	OPINION : ASKING	Questions.
(3)	P+	PROPOSAL : GIVING	Most usually a proposal about discussion procedure.
(4)	P−	PROPOSAL : ASKING	A proposal about discussion put in a form of a question.
(5)	I+	INFORMATION : GIVING	Specific facts usually to clarify statements.
(6)	I−	INFORMATION : ASKING	A request for information, or to clarify a discussion procedure.
(7)	EA+	ACADEMIC REFERENCE : GIVING	A quote or reference to some academic work.
(8)	EA−	ACADEMIC REFERENCE : ASKING	A question about a reference to academic work.
(9)	EAO+	ACADEMIC REFERENCE AND OPINION : GIVING	An opinion including reference to an academic source.
(10)	EAP+	ACADEMIC REFERENCE AND PROPOSAL : GIVING	A proposal to discuss in terms of quoted academic framework.
(11)	EE+	EXPERIENCE : GIVING	Reference to specific experience in schools.
(12)	EE−	EXPERIENCE : ASKING	Asking about specific experiences in schools.
(13)	EEO+	EXPERIENCE AND OPINION : GIVING	An opinion including a reference to experience.
(14)	EFO−	EXPERIENCE AND OPINION : ASKING	A question asking about an experience-based opinion.

Analysis by Model B

Precis II method

Precis I statements were shortened even further to produce Precis II. For this analysis statements were re-worded and re-ordered so that their meaning was conveyed as clearly and succinctly as possible.

The process of reduction and re-ordering from Precis I to Precis II is shown in Example 2.

Example 2

> Precis I
> 'This depends on amount of years a teacher has been teaching. A young teacher on first name terms . . . its rather difficult for them. They have first of all to get a position and then move downwards . . . older teachers yes.'
> reduces to Precis II
> 'Christian names depends on how long a teacher has been teaching: (it is) harder for young teachers than older teachers, have to get position and move down.'

Precis II statements were then classified according to Model B.

Model B
The interest of this model is the width and range of themes discussed under the general discussion topic. The concern was not so much with the actual views of the teachers about these themes but, simply, with the number and type of themes covered.

One or two categories of the Model were established before the discussions were studied. This was in order to discover if these aspects of the topic were raised at all. These categories were as follows:

(1) definitions of basic skills (or social/moral behaviour);
(2) definitions of Aims;
(3) justifications for choice of basic skills (or social/moral behaviour);
(4) justifications for choice of Aims.

Particular interest centred on definitions of aims in connection with the further work of the Project, but the nature of the discussants' justifications for their choice of aims was of interest as an indication of the factors which had influenced these choices.

Apart from these four categories the categories (as listed in Table 3 below) were chosen as a result of a study of the discussions. Statements dealing with a similar theme or aspect of the discussion topic were grouped together. It was found that similar themes were considered in all seven discussion groups. Themes about which only a few statements were made are not classified separately but included in the 'Non-classified' category.

The discussions proved to be more complex than had been anticipated and more themes were discussed than had been expected. For example, a preliminary reading revealed that the teachers rarely gave a simple definition of a basic skill, but more often gave a definition and a temporal order of several basic skills, or they attempted to balance the importance of several basic skills in relation to each other. These were classified in separate categories.

Table 2a: Frequency and percentage total contributions in each category: seven discussion groups combined

Symbol	Meaning	f	% of total statements
O+	Opinion: Giving	560	
			679 87.0
O−	Opinion: Asking	119	
P+	Proposal: Giving	27	
			41 5.0
P−	Proposal: Asking	14	
I+	Information: Giving	22	
			31 4.0
I−	Information: Asking	9	
EA+	Academic Reference: Giving	4	
EA−	Academic Reference: Asking	1	
			12 2.0
EAO+	Academic Reference and opinion: Giving	6	
EAP+	Academic Reference and proposal: Giving	1	
EE+	Experience: Giving	13	
EE−	Experience: Asking	3	
			18 2.0
EEO+	Experience and opinion: Giving	1	
EEO−	Experience and opinion: Asking	1	
N		781	100.0

Table 2b: Frequency order of categories

	Symbol	Order f
1	O+	560
2	O−	119
3	P+	27
4	I+	22
5	P−	14
6	EE+	93
7	I−	9
8	EAO+	6
9	EA+	4
10	EE−	3
11	EA−	1
12	EEO+	1
13	EEO−	1
14	EAP+	1
	N	781

Table 2c: Statements and Questions

	N	%
The total number of statements	634	81
The total number of questions	147	19

Having classified the statements into their respective themes it was then possible to judge the amount of attention devoted to each theme by counting the number of statements in each category.

As Model B categories are not exactly the same for the two sets of discussions, their detailed description is presented with the results for the relevant set of discussions (see Tables 3 and 7, below).

The results: I discussion of 'to develop the basic skills': model A
Table 2a below shows the number and percentage of total contributions in each category, for all seven groups discussing the 'Basic Skills' area of aims. Table 2b shows the frequency order of the categories, and 2c the proportion of statements and questions.

Discussion of the results
Tables 2a and 2b highlight a number of features of the discussions.

(a) Eighty-seven per cent of all contributions were expressions of opinion (category O+) or questions about opinions (O—). Whilst caution must be exercised throughout and it must be remembered that this analysis is of only seven discussions, the preponderance of opinion-giving is noteworthy. It would suggest a high level of confidence on the part of these group members, for the most part, complete strangers to one another, to offer their personal views as substantive data on which to arrive at a group judgment.

(b) Most contributions were statements (all categories coded +). Only 19 per cent were questions, (all categories coded —) and most of these were questions about opinions. This would indicate that the dialectic of discussion was conducted by a series of statements and counter statements rather than by a Socratic question and answer method. Perhaps it was felt that the latter style had too strong a flavour of the classroom to be suitable for discussion between colleagues

(c) Only two per cent of statements (the last four categories of Table 2a) made direct reference to the teachers' actual classroom experiences. It is difficult to understand why there are so few. This may be because the members of the groups assumed a common experience which they did not need to refer to explicitly.

(d) The small number of explicit references to theoretical works or empirical studies in education (two per cent), is difficult to account for. We do not know if this is because teachers are uninfluenced by such works in their thinking about aims, though there is evidence for this point of view, (Taylor, P. H., 1970) or whether the *style* of the discussion precludes specific references to academic sources. There is certainly evidence of an assumed common body of 'academic' material. Mentions of 'concrete stage', 'formal stage' or 'different stages of development' were fairly frequent and discussants seem to know that these terms are a reference to Piaget's developmental model, without it being necessary to quote his name. It would appear that this implicitly known body of academic works consists of writers studied by teachers during initial or further training. What seems to be missing in these discussions is any evidence of teachers' study of academic material which they consciously relate to their discussion of aims.

(e) The categories concerning experience or academic sources could be regarded as the 'factual' base of the discussion and it is interesting to see what a small proportion of the discussion is directly concerned with 'facts'. This could be due to the common training and experience of the discussants.

One possibility is that this analysis described a certain style of language behaviour. When groups of teachers are given a topic to discuss in this fashion it may be that they feel it should be discussed on the level of opinion and that it is inappropriate to bring in their own experiences or academic reading. This point is further discussed below. In this case the frequencies here might describe a 'register' of discussion. While these particular discussants happen to be teachers, we do not know if groups of lay people or members of different professions would have a similar 'style' based largely on opinions and positive statements when discussing aims in education.

Analysis by Model B
A general description of Model B has been given above. Table 3 below presents the detailed description of the Model B categories used to classify statements made in the 'Basic Skills' discussions.

Table 3: Classification: Model B

Symbol	Category Title	Example
A	Function and role of teacher	Our role is to create an interest in learning.
B	School organization and role of Head	Progressive schools do not stress schemes of work. I think their aims are indefinite.
C	Justications of Basic Skills	'Basic Skills are needed by children if they are not to be at a disadvantage in society.'

Table 3 continued

Symbol	Category Title	Example
D	Discussion procedures	'Shall we start by defining the Basic Skills?' 'What does everyone mean by the Basic Skills?'
D_1	Definitions (other than of the Basic Skills)	Wisdom is the ability to see the elements of a situation and be able to deal with it in a reasonable way.
E	Definitions Basic Skills	Writing is one of the basic skills. Reading is basic—everyone must learn to read.
F	Order of Aims (Aims/ Methods)*	In the Infants the first thing we must do is to let the children settle in before attempting to give out.
F_1	Relative Importance Aims (Aims/Methods)	We must not think only of book learning; it is also important to increase the child's activity and experience.
G	Definitions Aims	By end of Junior school the child should read, write and know some arithmetic.
G_1	Definitions: Aims/Methods*	Teachers stimulate interest to give children ideas to communicate.
H	Justification for Aims	(Aims to get children adaptable— so that they can easily accommodate to new situations, changes of job and so on) *'because they will have to do this a lot in the future.'*
H_1	Justification for Aims/ Methods	'Without this class teaching is impossible.'
J	Negative Aims (Aims/ Methods)	'Training and conditioning are against my aim of education.'
K	Influences on Aims (Aims/Methods)	'We must educate them so they can deal with secondary education.'
K_1	Influences on Basic Skills	'They cannot do the discovery mathematics until they can do the computation that emerges from their discoveries.'
L	Influences on the Child's Development	'A child's knowledge depends on home background and pre-school parental interest.'
L_1	Child development	'Infants are not just playing; they are fully engaged mentally the whole time. It is only gradually you get group play developing.'
NG	Non-classified	'Parents want success for their children in one form or another, but have little idea of how it is to be achieved.'

* Aims/Methods. This is used to indicate a statement which may equally refer to an aim or a method.

Table 4: Model B. The frequency and per cent of total statements in each category:
shown in order of descending frequency

Symbol	Category Title	Frequency of Statements	% of Total Statements
D	Discussion procedures	174	19
E	Definitions Basic Skills	100	11
G	Definitions of Aims	97	11
G_1	Definitions of Aims/Methods	75	8
D_1	Definitions (other than of Basic Skills)	61	7
K	Influences on Aims (Aims/Methods)	54	6
A	Function and role of the teacher	52	6
F_1	Relative Importance of Aims (Aims/Methods)	46	5
F	Order of Aims (Aims/Methods)	41	5
L	Influences on the Child's Development	38	4
C	Justifications for Basic Skills	31	3
H_1	Justifications for Aims/Methods	19	2
J	Negative Aims (Aims/Methods)	19	2
H	Justifications for Aims	15	2
L_1	Child Development	13	1
K_1	Influences on Basic Skills	12	1
B	School Organization and the Role of the Head	5	1
NC	Non-classified	65	7
N		917*	101

* There are a larger number of statements in Model B than in Model A. This is because one statement in Model A sometimes refers to more than one aspect of the discussion topic.

Discussion

It will be recalled that no guidance was given to the teachers on how to discuss the topic and in the light of this it is probable that the discussions do reflect the teachers' spontaneous reaction to the topic. The analysis of the discussions suggest the following points.

(1) An outstanding feature of the discussions was the large number of definitions given. Definitions of basic skills, aims, aims/methods and other definitions account altogether for 37 per cent of all statements. This may be due to the novelty of the topic. We may have expected teachers to have a fairly common set of definitions of their basic terms, but in fact they seemed to need to spend a large proportion of the time explicitly stating and defining them, indicating which meanings they had chosen from the possible range.

(2) Definitions of aims and aims/methods are related to a wide range of topics. Apart from direct justifications (Categories H and H_1) we find categories covering order of aims (F), relative importance of aims

(F_1), influences on aims and aims/methods (K_1), negative aims (J). Each of these had a relatively small number of statements.

(3) The definitions of basic skills, however, were connected with only two other issues. These were direct justifications (C) and influences on basic skills (K_1), both of which had a very small number of statements.

(4) The small number of direct justifications of aims, aims/methods and basic skills strengthens the impression of self confidence which has been noted above (Table 4). Participants did not feel the need to give reasons for their choice of aims or basic skills. But some of the statements included in categories K and L may have been indirect justifications. Such statements, from category K, as 'the secondary school must surely influence what we teach' or 'how does size of school influence what we teach' may not be very different from 'we must bring the child up to a certain level and develop his character so that he leaves as a mature individual' (from category H). It is the direct emphasis in the latter (H) statement which makes it a clear justification. But K and L statements could be regarded as a reason for aims choices, and in this sense as a form of justification.

(5) While any detailed consideration of teaching methods is beyond the scope of this discussion, the category of statements concerning putting aims into practice is fairly large (A: six per cent). These are not statements of detailed teaching methods but are general lines of approach. An example of an 'A' type statement is 'one of our aims is to diagnose the need of every child. *Meeting parents helps to do this better.*' The underlined sentence represents an A statement. Such statements emphasize the practical bias of teachers by linking aims to practice.

(6) It will be noted that the category dealing with child development (L) is rather smaller than the category containing statements about the influences on child development (L_1). This confirms the impression that the teachers' interest is practical and active and this leads them to a consideration of the factors which hinder or advance child development rather than a theoretical description of child development as such.

(7) The largest category of statements is not directly concerned with the topic discussed but is category D—Discussion Procedure—with 19 per cent of statements. The reason for this high proportion of procedural statements could be that the groups were meeting for its first time when discussing this topic. They therefore had no established

rules of procedure and it is interesting to see that such a large proportion of statements were needed to set up a frame-work or, as Walker (1971) refers to it, 'a platform' within which the discussion could proceed. It is not possible to say if the large number of procedural statements could be due to lack of familiarity with *discussion technique* or lack of familiarity with the discussion *topic*.

At this time the teachers had in all probability not discussed aims explicitly before and the novelty of the topic may have meant they were particularly unsure of the scope and approach to the discussion. The large number of procedural statements could be a reflection of their uncertainty about the scope of the discussion and the amount of attention required for the different aspects of the topic. It seems reasonable to suggest that had the discussants been more familiar with the topic they may have been able to switch from one aspect of it to another and would have realized when an aspect was 'finished' and which new aspect followed on 'naturally'. On the other hand un-familiarity with discussion as a means of interaction could lead to hesitancy about procedure and result in a large number of statements which deal with problems of this type.

In the absence of any comparative ratios of 'procedure' to 'content' for other types of people and other topics it is not possible to decide whether this high proportion of procedural statements represents any special sort of behaviour by these groups of teachers.

Time Analysis: Model B
Introduction
One of the interesting aspects of the discussions was the change in themes discussed over the course of the meetings. Themes were introduced, discussed and then dropped. A new theme would be taken up and dropped in its turn. Sometimes a previous theme would be re-introduced after having been left for a time. Thus the discussions have an inter-weaving of themes over time. A detailed description of this inter-play of themes was beyond the techniques and resources available, but a crude attempt to describe the flow of discussion was essayed. This involved comparing statements made in the first half of the discussion with those made in the second half.

Method
Each separate statement made was numbered in order of utterance. Those statements with a low number were made early in the discussion, while those with a high number were made later. For the purpose of

the time analysis the total number of statements in a discussion was divided by two. Statements made in the first half of the discussion were those with the lower numbers, and the statements made in the later half of the discussion had the higher numbers. The statements in each of the categories occurring in each half of the discussion were noted, and the differences in frequency in each category for the first and second halves of the discussion was tested to determine if they were greater than chance.

Results

Table 5 below shows the results of this analysis for all seven groups combined.

Table 5: Comparison of the per cent of statements in each half of the discussion

CATEGORIES WITH LARGE PER CENT OF STATEMENTS IN THE FIRST HALF		CATEGORIES WITH LARGE PER CENT OF STATEMENTS IN THE SECOND HALF	
Symbol	*Category Title*	*Symbol*	*Category Title*
B	School organization and role of Head	A*	Function and role of teacher
D**	Discussion procedures	C	Justifications of Basic Skills
E**	Definition Basic Skills	D_1	Definitions (other than of the Basic Skills)
F**	Order of Aims (Aims/ Methods)	G**	Definitions of Aims
F_1**	Relative Importance Aims (Aims/Methods)	G_1**	Definitions of Aims/ Methods
H_1	Justification for Aims/ Methods	H	Justification for Aims
J	Negative Aims (Aims/ Methods)	K**	Influence on Aims (Aims/Methods)
K_1	Influences on Basic Skills	L	Influences on the Child's Development
		L_1	Child development

** = t sig. at ·01 per cent level.
 * = t sig. at ·05 per cent level.

Discussion of the results

(i) As we would expect, the first half of the discussion contains significantly more procedural statements than the second half; 23 per cent of the contributions in the first half of the discussion were procedural, whereas such statements represent 16 per cent of contributions to the second half of the discussion.

(ii) Definitions of basic skills (E) are significantly more frequent in the first half of the discussion but definitions of aims and aims/methods are more frequent in the second half. It seems that teachers approached the topic by defining basic skills and then moved on to define aims.

(iii) It is of interest to note, however, that categories F (order of aims), and F_1 (relative importance of aims), were larger in the first half of the discussion. It seems as if that in the first half, aims statements were made in connection with their order or the balance between different aims.

(iv) In the second half of the discussion categories L (influences on child development) and K (influences on aims) were found to be significantly larger. This would suggest that, in this half of the discussion, aims definitions were made in relation to influences on child development or wider academic and social influences on the choice of aims. The aims in the first half of the discussion were those associated with the basic skills and would tend therefore to have a hierarchical structure to some extent. The aims defined in the second half of the discussion are discussed in relation to encouraging normal child development and with reference to the demand of secondary education and the wider community.

(v) The category of statements dealing with the teachers' function (A) is larger in the second half. This may indicate that teachers grew more confident as the discussion progressed and felt capable of relating the more theoretical points raised to their actual classroom practice.

(vi) Definitions of terms other than basic skills occur in both halves of the discussion, slightly more in the second half (but not significantly so). It seems that terms were defined as they were introduced into the discussion. The slight predominance of such definitions in the second half might suggest a tendency for the discussants to move towards the obscurer aspects of the topic nearer the end of the discussion. After the relatively straight-forward task of defining basic skills was completed, the less straight-forward aspects were explored, involving more unusual concepts and vocabulary.

Results II: Discussion of 'to Foster Social and Moral Development'

Introduction

The last of the four topics discussed by the groups was 'to foster social and moral development'. For this study three groups out of the seven were analysed. The précis-methods are identical to those described in Section III and IVA for the 'Basic Skills' discussions. The results are presented for all three groups combined. As in the previous discussion, the differences between the pooled results and individual groups were not greater than would be expected by chance.

ANALYSIS BY MODEL A

Social and Moral Development
Classification (Model A): three groups combined

Table 6a: Frequency and Percentage of Contributions in Each Category: 3 Groups Combined

Table 6b: Order of Frequency of Statements in Each Category

Symbol	Title	Freq.	% of Total Statements	Statement Type Symbol		Freq.
O+	OPINION: GIVING	222 ⎫		1	O+	222
		⎬ 284	83·0			
O−	OPINION: ASKING	62 ⎭		2	O−	62
P+	PROPOSAL: GIVING	8 ⎫		3	EEO+	15
		⎬ 10	3·0	4	EE+	12
P−	PROPOSAL: ASKING	2 ⎭		5	EA+	
I+	INFORMATION: GIVING	3 ⎫				
		⎬ 5	2·0	6	P+	8
I−	INFORMATION: ASKING	2 ⎭				
EA+	ACADEMIC REFERENCE: GIVING	.. 12 ⎫		7	I+	3
		⎬ 13	4·0			
EAO+	ACADEMIC REFERENCE AND OPINION: GIVING	1 ⎭		8	I−	2
				9	EAo+	1
EE+	EXPERIENCE: GIVING	12 ⎫		10	EE−	1
EE−	EXPERIENCE: ASKING	1 ⎬ 28	8·0			
EEO+	EXPERIENCE AND OPINION: GIVING	15 ⎭				
		340	**100·0**		**N**	**340**

Table 6c.	Total statements	270=80%
	Total questions	67=20%

Discussion

(1) Eighty-four per cent of all contributions are opinions or questions about opinions, and opinion-stating appears to have been the overall style of the discussion. The far smaller proportion of questions (20 per cent) suggests that the discussants carried out the argument by a series of statements of opinion rather than by a dialectic of question and answer.

(2) References to personal experiences accounted for eight per cent of contributions. This relatively large proportion may be due to the

lack of clarity of the concepts in the social and moral field. This may have led the discussants to illustrate the particular aspect of a concept with which they were concerned, by reference to examples from practical experience.

(3) References to academic sources accounted for four per cent of all contributions. This is far smaller than the proportion of opinions stated and would imply that, in their consideration of aims in the social and moral field, the teachers did not take into consideration the results of academic studies to any large extent.

Analysis by Model B

Classification by Model B

For the analysis of the topic 'to foster social and moral development', the same categories were used in Model B so far as they were applicable to the themes discussed. One interesting additional category (F_2) was required to classify a group of statements dealing with the demands of conflicting moral or social aims (such as 'group cohesion' conflicting with the aims of 'encouraging individuality' or 'independence'). This problem had not arisen in the 'Basic Skills' discussions and the new category, F_2, was established for this type of statement. The other categories were simply reworded to cover the change in subject matter, thus category C became 'justifications for social and moral behaviour' and category E became 'definitions of social and moral behaviour'. The full list of the reworded categories is shown in Table 7 with the frequencies of statements in each one.

Results

The results are presented in Table 7.

Discussion

(1) Thirty-one per cent of all contributions to the discussions were definitions of one kind or another. These included definitions of aims, aims/methods, social and moral behaviour. Although a certain degree of ambiguity and imprecision of terminology would be expected in this topic, the proportion of definitions is not, in fact, much different from the 'Basic Skills' discussions. It will be seen that the proportion of definitions other than of aims and of social and moral behaviour is very small. This may indicate that the discussion was more narrowly concentrated than the 'Basic Skills' discussions had been, but may also be due to the fact that by the time the topic of social and moral develop-

Table 7: *Order of size of categories: 3 discussion groups combined*

Symbol	Category Title	Frequency of Statements	% of Total Statements
A	Function and Role of teacher	72	15·0
E	Definitions of Moral and Social Behaviour	70	15·0
G	Definitions of Aims	54	11·0
K	Influences on Aims and Aims/Methods	35	7·0
F_2	Conflicting Aims	31	7·0
D	Procedure	25	5·0
L	Influences in Child Development	23	5·0
J	Negative Aims	22	5·0
L_1	Child's Development	22	5·0
G_1	Definitions of Aims/Methods	22	5·0
B	Role of Head in Social and Moral Education	18	4·0
C	Justification for Social and Moral Behaviour	18	4·0
H_2	Justification Order Moral/Social Behaviour	11	2·0
F_1	Relative Importance of Aims (Aims/Methods)	10	2·0
F	Order of Aims (Aims/Methods)	6	1·0
K_1	Influences on Moral and Social Behaviour	5	1·0
J_1	Negative results	3	1·0
H	Justification for Aims	3	1·0
D_1	Definitions of terms (not Moral/Social Behaviour)	2	(—1·0)
NC		20	4·0
	TOTAL	472	

ment was discussed the members of the groups were familiar with the general educational terms used.

(2) The discussions had a practical tone. One of the largest categories was A, which includes statements on the role and function of the teacher in social and moral education. This practical approach was further emphasized by the high proportion of statements dealing with conflicting aims. For it is in practice that the problem of balance between different aims will arise and the teacher may well find difficulty in reconciling such aims in the classroom situation.

(3) It will be seen that only three per cent of the contributions are concerned with the relative order or importance of aims. This suggests that social and moral development is seen as non-hierarchial, in that development does not proceed on the basis of previous knowledge as it does to some extent in the teaching of the basic skills.

(4) The relatively large proportion of statements concerned with

c

child development and the influences upon it (categories L and L_1: 10 per cent), would suggest that the teachers saw social and moral behaviour in terms of child development and maturation rather than in terms of a subject hierarchy.

Time Analysis: Model B
Method

The method for this analysis is the same as for the previous set of discussions, ('Basic Skills'), which is described above. The total number of contributions was divided in two. The number of contributions in each category was found for the first and second half of the discussion: t-tests were carried out to determine if the differences in frequency between the two halves was greater than would be expected by chance. The results of this analysis are shown in Table 8.

Table 8: Categories larger in the first or second half of the discussion

Categories Larger % First Half		Categories Larger % Second Half	
Symbol	Category Title	Symbol	Category Title
C	Justification for Social and Moral Behaviour	A	Function and Role of teacher
D*	Procedure	B	Moral Education
D_1	Definition of terms (not Moral/Social Behaviour)	F	Order of Aims and Methods
E*	Definition Basic Skills	F_1	Importance of Aims and Methods
F_2*	Conflicting Aims	G	Definitions of Aims
J_1	Negative results	G_1**	Aims/Methods
K_1	Influences on Moral and Social Behaviour	H	Justification for Aims
L	Influences on Child Development	H_2	Justification Order Moral/Social Behaviour
L_1	Child's development	J	Negative Aims and Methods
		K	Influences on Aims and Aims/Methods

* =difference sig. at ·05 level.
** =difference sig. at ·01 level.

Discussion of the results

(1) There are three categories which are significantly larger in the first half than in the second. These are: definitions of social and moral behaviour (E); procedure (D); and conflicting aims (F_2). The members of the groups preferred to define social and moral behaviour before

aims were stated. This is presumably to clarify the terms used in stating the aims.

(2) The problem of conflicting social and moral aims was considered in the first half of the discussion. It would appear that the definition of aims in the first half of the discussion were considered in relation to the problems of conflict, but this did not occur with definitions of aims made in the second half of the discussions.

(3) There is one category of statements which is significantly larger in the second half of the discussion. This is the definition of Aims/Methods (G_1). It may be that this type of statement has a somewhat more practical bias than a straight-forward definition of Aims, so that the increase in such statements in the second half of the discussion may suggest that the interest of the members took a more directly practical turn as the discussion proceeded. This impression is strengthened by the larger number of statements occurring in the second half in category A, (Role and Function of the Teacher in Social and Moral Development), which, while it does not reach significance, is quite large.

(4) As would be expected, procedural matters were largely dealt with in the first half of the discussion. In fact only four statements were made in the second half which dealt with procedure.

III Comparison of the Two Sets of Aims Discussions

The results presented in this paper are based on a précis of a series of discussions about aims conducted by primary school teachers. For both topics the results of the separate discussion groups are combined. The results of the 'Basic Skills' were based on seven separate groups of discussions and the results of the 'To Foster Social and Moral Development' discussions were based on three separate groups.

The pooled results for Model B analysis for both topics were compared with the totals for the separate discussion groups. As explained in the text, in no instance were the differences in number of contributions to a category between the individual group and the pooled totals greater than would be expected by chance. This indicates that the groups approached both topics in a similar fashion. This useful result suggests that none of the discussion groups was dominated by on outstanding ('charismatic') individual who was able to turn the discussion in a direction of his or her own interest. (The presence of a charismatic individual is not unusual and often makes the analysis of discussions of doubtful value.) In the case of the groups analysed in this present study it would seem that the similarity of the results for the separate groups and the norm indicates that the discussions were based on group interests, as it would be unlikely that a dominant individual would skew the discussion in the same direction for every group.

In view of the homogeneity of the groups it was felt legitimate to compare the combined results for both discussion topics although these results are not based on the same number of groups in both cases. The three groups analysed for the 'Social and Moral Development' discussions are included along with the seven groups analysed for the 'Basic Skills' discussions. As no difference was found between the seven groups in their discussions of 'Basic Skills. it was felt justifiable to assume that this would be the case for the 'Social and Moral Development' discussions. Therefore, in this summary, direct comparisons are made between the results for the two topics.

Model A

Model A gives a description of the style of discussion.

(1) The overwhelming type of contribution was opinion-stating or asking. Over 80 per cent of contributions, in both topics, were of this kind.

(2) The discussions of the topic 'To Foster Social and Moral Development' contained a larger proportion of 'opinion' questions than did the discussions of the 'Basic Skills'. But in both cases the total proportion of questions of all kinds to non-questions was about the same. The relatively small proportion of questions in each topic-discussion suggests that the style of any aims discussion is one of opinion and counter opinion and that this style is not affected by the aim under discussion.

(3) Both topics produced only a small proportion of references to academic material. It will be recalled that two per cent of total contributions to the 'Basic Skills' discussions were such references, and four per cent of contributions to the 'Foster Social and Moral Development' discussions. The increased proportion of statements of this type in the latter discussion is hard to account for and may be due to several causes. Lack of confidence in achieving social and moral aims may have led teachers to seek guidance from authoritative works. Lack of concensus about aims in the social and moral sphere may have encouraged reference to academic works to support aims choices. However, in neither discussion does it appear that academic sources played a large part in the teachers' consideration of aims.

(4) The small number of references to direct personal experiences in the 'Basic Skills' discussions was surprising. From later information obtained from members of the discussion groups it would appear that the teachers in the groups felt that such material was unsuitable for a discussion about aims. This view might be the result of the design of teacher-training courses where aims are considered as part of 'philosophy and theory' and as such seen as in some way opposed to 'practice'. Thus in an aims discussion teachers might feel it was unsuitable to quote practical examples from their teaching experiences. This finds support from the transcripts of the discussions where a flavour of unsophisticated 'philosophizing' appears. For example,

'. . . Knowledge, I define as a sort of three dimensional map, as it has height as well as breadth.'
'I think of knowledge as what's up here, the facts have all been collected and these increase.'
'I can't see how you can put dimensions to knowledge.'

There was however, a larger percentage of references to experience in the 'To Foster Social and Moral Development' discussions (eight per cent). It is possible that in this series of discussions the group members realized the value of explicit references to their own experiences when considering aims. On the whole the group showed a greater concern for the empirical basis of their opinions than they had done in the basic skills discussions, and for placing these within a philosophic framework. Viewed from this aspect, the later discussions might perhaps be considered more sophisticated.

Model B
Model B shows the different themes of the topic which were discussed by the groups. Each category in Model B represents a different aspect of the topic and the categories combined represent a total 'view' of the topic as seen by the groups. No knowledge was available beforehand of how the teachers would approach a discussion of aims and what they would assume could be included in it. Most of the categories for analysis were established after scrutiny of the transcripts.

There were 17 categories in both the discussions of 'Basic Skills' and 'To Foster Social and Moral Development'. These 17 categories accounted for 96 per cent of all the statements made, the other four per cent of statements were of such a diverse nature that it was not possible to locate them in any category and it was hardly worthwhile establishing categories containing only one or two statements.

The number of categories may seem large but we know of no material with which comparisons can be made.

While both discussions had the same number of categories, there was one category in each discussion which had no parallel in the other. The 'Basic Skills' had a category which included a small number of statements concerned with the justifications for an order of teaching basic skills (H_3): no such theme was raised in the discussion of 'To Foster Social and Moral Development'. This discussion, however, contained a category of statements dealing with the possible conflict of aims (F_2), which had not been discussed at all in the 'Basic Skills' discussions. Apart from these two categories it will be seen that the themes discussed were similar for each of the topics.

From Tables 4 and 7 it will be noticed that there is a good deal of variation in the number of statements in each category between the two discussion topics. This, it is suggested, is an indication of the amount of interest in the aspect of the topic and the difference in the proportion of total statements in similar categories for the two discussion topics are assumed, therefore, to represent differences of interest in the themes.

Some of the differences in the proportion of statements in a category between the two discussions might also be the result of differences in subject matter, other differences are more likely to be due to the increased familiarity of the discussants with the process of discussing aims.

There are some categories which are of equal proportion in both sets of discussions and it is possible that these represent the common ground of any discussion of aims, irrespective of the specific aims which are discussed.

(1) The largest difference in category which may be due to differences in subject is the increased proportion of statements concerning the role and function of the teacher in social and moral development, as compared with the role and function of the teacher in the acquisition of the basic skills. The difference in proportion between the two discussion topics is nine per cent. It is possible that the members of the discussions considered that the teacher had more of an active role in fostering social and moral development than in the teaching of the basic skills; or it may reflect a lower level of confidence in the proper role of the teacher in fostering social and moral development.

A much smaller but interesting difference between the two topics is the difference in the proportion of statements concerning the Role of the Head and the Organization of the School in fostering the social and moral development of the children and in teaching the basic skills. This aspect of the topic was hardly discussed in connection with the 'Basic Skills' but four per cent of the statements in the 'To Foster Social and Moral Development' discussions are on this theme. This may suggest that the teachers involved in the discussion saw the Head Teacher and the wider school organization as having a greater part to play in social and moral development than in teaching of the basic skills, which appear to be seen largely as a classroom activity.

(2) The relationship between different aims is considered rather differently in the two discussions. In the 'Basic Skills' discussions the relationship is seen as one of the optimum order of presentation or of the relative importance of aims. Ten per cent of the total statements were concerned with these aspects. In the discussions on 'To Foster Social and Moral Development' the relationship is seen more often in terms of conflict and the achievement of some aims is seen as possibly hindering the achievement of other aims. Seven per cent of total statements in the discussion were concerned with the problem of a conflict of aims.

(3) The proportion of references to child development and influences on child development varies in each of the two sets of discussions. There is a difference of five per cent between each set of discussions which may reflect the degree of 'child centredness' of the two topics. Whereas the 'Basic Skills' aims appear to be seen as determined by the needs of the subjects to be learned, the social and moral aspects of development are seen to be influenced to a far greater extent by the development of the child and by what the teacher feels is possible at a given age or level of development.

(4) The difference in the proportion of procedural statements in each of the sets of discussions is most marked. It is suggested that this difference (14 per cent) is due not to the difference in the context of the two topics discussed, but is rather due to the order in which they were discussed. It is possible that the large proportion of procedural statements in the 'Basic Skills' discussion was due to this being the first of the series. At this time the members of the discussion groups were discussing aims for the first time and the large proportion of procedural aims may have reflected their lack of familiarity both with discussion techniques and with the problems of discussing aims. By the time they came to discuss 'To Foster Social and Moral Development' the discussants had had practice in discussing aims. The smaller

proportion of procedural statements in this discussion strongly suggests that by this time a procedural framework for the discussion had been established and so there was far less need to make explicit statements referring to procedure. Further practice in discussing aims had enabled the discussants to realize the issues which were fruitfully considered, rendering less need for explicit statements concerning the flow of discussion.

(5) The similarities in proportion of total statements in some of the categories is as interesting as the differences.

The categories which had similar proportions of statements for both of the topics discussed include definitions of aims, justifications for aims and influences on aims. Definitions accounted for about 30 per cent of statements in both sets of discussions. This is perhaps because it was something of a novelty for the group members to consider aims. On the other hand, only a small proportion (six to seven per cent) of the statements in each discussion were concerned with justifying aims choices directly, although it is possible that aims choices were justified indirectly in statements about child development.

Summary
The analysis of the two sets of discussions suggest that groups of teachers discuss aims largely in terms of opinion. The small proportion of questions in the discussions suggests that opinions were not challenged by questioning but rather by counter statement.

Both sets of discussions contained only a small proportion of direct references to academic works or to teaching experiences, although the proportion was larger in the later set of discussions ('Social/Moral Development') than in the earlier set of discussions ('Basic Skills').

In both sets of discussion group members covered 17 themes or subtopics under the general discussion topic. The largest proportion of statements in both sets of discussions were definitions of one kind or another. The 'Social/Moral Development' discussions tended to have a larger proportion of statements dealing with the practical implication of aims choices (Role of teacher, Role of Head and School organization) than the 'Basic Skills' discussions.

This is an encouraging development and it is possible that the series of aims discussions represent a learning process during which the group members clarified their aims and their views of the relation of aims to classroom and school practices.

It would appear from this study that a teacher's aims could be influenced by her experiences with children. In turn her aims could influence her classroom practices. Thus aims are not static, but are likely to be modified in the light of a deeper understanding of children and of teaching. In view of the dynamic relationship between aims and practice it could well be fruitful if teachers, at least from time to time throughout their careers, made a conscious examination of their aims and of the relation of their aims to their general style of teaching.

References

ASHTON, P. M., KNEEN, P., DAVIES, F. R., and HOLLEY, B. J. (1974) *The Aims of Primary Education*. London: Macmillan.

BALES, R. F. (1951) *Interaction Process Analysis*. Cambridge, Mass.: Addison-Wesley.

STONE, P. J. *et al.* (1966) *The General Inquirer*. Cambridge, Mass.: MIT Press.

TAYLOR, P. H. (1970) *How Teachers Plan Their Courses*. Slough: NFER.

WALKER, D. F. (1971). 'A naturalistic model for curriculum development', *School. Rev.*, 80, 1, 51–65.

APPENDIX 1

Examples of Modern A Type of Statements

Opinions

Opinion Giving

. . . the general attitude to me means that we are going to turn out very stereotyped children . . . they are going to be very efficient and very knowledgeable . . . but . . . if we carry through our aims they are going to be a bit puddeny . . . going to come out in a pattern, very moulded, beautiful . . . no trouble to anybody.

. . . we are dealing with individuals, we can't turn children out exactly the same . . . whether you teach 40 individuals to read, write . . . doesn't mean you want to turn out 40 identical children at the end of the year.

. . . you said that the troubles we have in society are because educators . . . have had a negative approach and have failed . . . I don't think educators . . . from the turn of the century and upwards have been negative, . . . I think it's a lot more to do with society . . . and mass advertising and media like this rather than education.

. . . he's got to conform to a set of values of society as a whole, not to a small school society, although it begins in the school ... to conform to the majority opinion of good and bad in society. Not to minority extreme. ...

Opinion Asking

Are you ... implying ... that ... social training is an incidental ... that we must not put it on the timetable as a subject.

... the crux of the situation is ... how do you educate your children to live in a society that has been formed for them.

Could you clarify the communities ... do you mean communities within the society or different societies?

Academic References

... I think Michael Duane said once that, you know, adults interfere too much ... with children and it happens in infant schools. I think adults, parents tend to impress their adult concepts upon the children.

... a chap called Dearden of London ... written a book on, a philosophy of Primary Education produces and I think this might be a good framework to bring. ... He contends there are just three main aims: ... first aim is forms of understanding to be transmitted, the second one is, the basic intellectual skills; the third one is the basic social skills ... of personal relationship and all three are absolutely essential to each other.

... are we to assume that Piaget is right when he said—we get conceptual development at certain well-defined stages? Or could we push this along a little bit in our work by a greater amount of perceptive work?

This is a philosophical question. Professor Jeffreys said What is the difference between I know Mr Marsh, I know Mr Heslop? I know both of them. ... Mr Marsh because I've met him today ... Mr Heslop in an entirely different way, my knowledge of him is different ... I know him at certain personal levels and it's that sort of knowledge that I am thinking is the one worthwhile, not the one of just today ... it's this definition of knowing that ... is ... important.

... that immediately brought to my mind this novel of William Golding's ... they achieve their own social development in that ... sort of degeneration.

... in the film ... when Helen Keller felt the water and it registered for the first time ... a marvellous example of how the concept happening ... this is the sort of. ...

References to Experiences

... I wouldn't agree with this at all ... but this ... depends on our own background and experience when we've been teaching. At the moment in my school I have children from some 55 different Primary schools, or is it now 56 ... and these children ... are starting life in a completely new community and ... the social aspect of their education is completely the most important thing we have to do. There is nothing else. In my previous school ... I had about 1,100 Juniors and Infants ... for any poor unfortunate infant who had joined a community of this size we had to take special care of the individual. ...

... in my experience one of the disadvantages with a child's inability to learn is that the home background has forced too much of an adult responsibility upon some children before they are ready for it.

... before we blame the secondary schools, let's examine our own primary schools aims.

... one frequently meets well-intentioned primary school heads, who say categorically you cannot teach them anything until they can read. They cannot do discovery mathematics until they can do the necessary computation that emerges from the discovery.

I think of one particular girl that does this at the moment, she is very very shy but she produces a beautiful piece of poetry.

... so many children ... these days who are not socially confident, they have been rather restricted in their home backgrounds and until they are socially confident they are not in a learning situation.

There are times, when you haven't got the time at that moment, to give an explanation.

Yes I know Chelmsley Wood, I've taught in schools ... where you get children from different areas ... social training is incidental, surely a good teacher is practising this from 9 till 4 every day.

Information: Giving and Asking

Middle School in this area would be 13.

In Birmingham there is no Middle School.
What was the second part of the group leader's suggestion?

Proposals: Giving and Asking
. . . are going to have to very carefully define what we mean by basic
skills as applied to 12-year-olds for example.

. . . might be useful if we looked at the end of the Primary school stage
and tried to state what we hope to achieve . . . as a way of rounding off
this discussion, under the various headings that we have mentioned.

x44's way of describing the word knowledge is very interesting and I
wondered if anyone would like to add to this?

An example of original transcript from a section of a discussion

Another thing that strikes me is their ability to obey and understand a
rule, if they are going to be individuals and just self-centred one of the
things we've got to try and do is to show them, impose on them perhaps,
rules, which they will eventually come to see the necessity of, they will
have to obey a rule and everybody will obey the rule for the benefit of
everybody . . . which at the start they find very difficult.
    Erm . . . isn't it true that in the past we've felt that erm . . . a child's
academic levels, er . . . were so important that if children were successful in this direction that the school had performed its function but erm,
there is the feeling now that er to produce a balanced person; to fulfil a
part in life as an adult successfully, er it is necessary to provide social
training throughout school and that this should be thought of particularly as something that has to be done and not an incidental thing that
is fostered as it crops up . . . in other words, if I could just finish, erm,
education is a balanced thing and erm and it is for children when they
become adults to fit successfully into society and be able to cope with
life's problems and also to attain happiness because they are socially
well adjusted.
    Do people think that we ought to teach a subject like Physics at the
top of the junior school, is it really necessary to do formal teaching of
that kind, of how people live together and were er . . . how er . . . the

community is administered, served by various people such as the . . . is that something that we ought to teach in the junior school?

While I think there may be some point in what you say, I dislike thinking too much upon the terms of teaching, I prefer to think of education and in the junior school situations in which the children can learn for themselves and I think we already do have many situations in which children can learn sort of social interplay—we can have small committees to run various things, to get a play together or to decorate a wall of the room and in this way children can learn to work together and this is part of their social development isn't it, this is what social development means, it's learning to live and work with people and to gain some benefit from it. I think we should think more about situation training than actual teaching. I mean this is my philosophy throughout the whole of the junior school actually. . . . I mean particularly in this case.

I think children . . . a lot of the social development of children can be achieved too when they are playing games, don't you think that playing games together is very good social training?

I'd just like to comment on that because it's very interesting here when we first started our junior school, the children in the playground just sort of stood about and looked for trouble, and they didn't know actually how to play games together and they had to be taught, we actually had to teach them games which they could play together . . . very interesting that.

(Interruption . . . two speakers together . . .)

I think this was . . . this was true you see. . . .

A Study of the Emphasis Given by Teachers of Different Age Groups to Aims in Primary Education

P. H. Taylor (University of Birmingham)
B. J. Holley (University of Hull)

Introduction

This study was undertaken as part of the Aims of Primary Education Project (1974) in which a central feature was the rating by a national sample of teachers of 72 aims (see Appendix I) developed after long discussion with practising teachers. In their ratings teachers were asked to 'have in mind' children in their own school 'in the middle range of ability . . . at the end of their primary education'. From these teachers' ratings was derived information about the 'ultimate' objectives of primary education as perceived by teachers at various levels in primary schools. Additional surveys elicited views on the same aims from teachers in secondary schools, who receive the 'products' of primary education, and from lecturers in colleges of education who educate intending primary school teachers and through them have some influence on the process of education in primary schools.

These major surveys were concerned with the 'ultimate' objectives of primary education, with what a child should be, should do, or should be capable of doing at the end of his primary school career. However, further questions arise about the more *proximate* objectives held to be important for each of the sub-stages within primary education. In particular, are the various aims emphasized differently for different age groups of pupils? If so, which aims are emphasized relatively more at which ages, and which relatively less?

It is the purpose of this supplementary study to provide some answers to these questions.

46

Scope and Method

All the schools which were sampled in the larger study were also asked to distribute a questionnaire containing the 72 aims to one teacher of each of the age groups five, seven, nine and 11. These ages were chosen as representing (i) the initial stage of primary education; (ii) the end of infant education or First School as it is increasingly being called, and the beginning of junior education where important changes sometimes take place in the style and purpose of teaching; (iii) the mid-period of education in the junior school, when neither transfer from an infant school or department nor transfer from primary to secondary education looms large in the eyes of teacher or pupils; and (iv) the final stage of primary education.

Each respondent was asked to assess the extent to which he or she contributed to the attainment of each of the 72 aims in his or her teaching. The following 3-point scale was to be used for responses:

I contribute to this aim to a considerable extent—3
I contribute to this aim to a moderate extent   —2
I contribute to this aim very little, if at all   —1

In total, 131 teachers of five-year-olds, 136 of seven-year-olds, 121 of nine-year-olds and 131 of 11-year-olds responded. Since the purpose of this survey was to discover the differences if any in emphasis between the various stages of primary education, teachers were not asked to supply biographical or other information.

The background of consensus

Before turning to a consideration of differences between groups in the emphasis placed upon each aim it is important to stress the extent to which there is a considerable degree of agreement about the importance or unimportance of certain aims and, indeed, about the relative positions of aims rated. An attempt was made to assess the degree to which teachers of each age group agree with teachers of the other age groups in their overall *ordering* of the 72 aims by a straightforward correlation method and the results are presented in Table 1. The following procedure was used: Firstly the mean rating on each item for each group was computed, then for each group an order for the items was established using the mean rating as criterion. (See Appendix 2 for means for all 72 aims). Thus, for example, the highest mean for teachers of seven-year-olds was 2·95 (item 58: the child should be happy, cheerful and well balanced); this was accorded rank 1. The next highest (item 13: the child should find enjoyment in a variety of aspects

of schoolwork etc.) at 2·86 was accorded the rank 2 . . . and so on down
to the lowest mean 1·05 (item 68: the child should be able to conduct a
simple conversation in a foreign language) which was accorded rank 72.
The same procedure was used for each of the four groups. Spearman's
rank correlation coefficient was then computed between each pair of
groups.

Table 1: Spearman's rank correlation coefficients based on ranked mean ratings of aims

	5-year-olds	7-year-olds	9-year-olds
7-year-olds	·948		
9-year-olds	·787	·920	
11-year-olds	·760	·892	·966

Two features of this correlation are worthy of note; firstly the rank
correlation coefficients are consistently high. Even in comparing mean
ratings of items for teachers of five-year-olds with the corresponding
mean ratings for teachers of 11-year-olds the rank orders of the means
closely correspond with one another. The probability of such a coefficient appearing by chance is less than 1 in 10,000. Secondly, the
degree of agreement (as measured by the rank correlation coefficient) is
greater, the closer together are the two age groups under consideration
—a result which accords with common sense expectations and suggests
some continuity of purpose from stage to stage in primary education.

In terms of individual items, of the 10 most highly emphasized at
age five, no fewer than six appeared in the 10 most highly emphasized
at each of the other ages. Correspondingly, five items of the 10 given
least emphasis at age five are given very low relative emphasis at all
other ages.

The aims which consistently appear in the 'top ten' are:

58. The child should be happy, cheerful and well balanced;

13. The child should find enjoyment in a variety of aspects of school
work and gain satisfaction from his own achievements;

25. The child should be careful with and respectful of both his own
and other people's property;

26. The child should be able to read with understanding material
appropriate to his age group and interests;

12. The child should be able to read fluently and accurately at
minimum reading age of 11;

24. The child should be beginning to acquire a set of moral values on
which to base his own behaviour; for example honesty, sincerity,
personal responsibility.

Teachers of all four age groups consider that they make a considerable contribution to the attainment of these aims. On the other hand all four groups consider that they make little or no contribution to the following five aims:

68. The child should be able to conduct a simple conversation in a foreign language;
49. The child should be able to play a musical instrument such as a recorder, violin, guitar;
61. The child should have some knowledge of the beliefs of major world religions other than Christianity;
35. The child should have ordered subject knowledge in, for example history, geography;
41. The child should know the basic facts of sex and reproduction.

It must be remembered that the teachers in this instance were asked to assess *their own contribution* to the achievement of these aims; they were not being asked which were important or desirable. Given the response required of teachers the difference between the two lists of items presented above appears to be one of generality. Those aims to which teachers of all age groups make a considerable contribution are concerned with general, social and moral attributes and the basic skill of reading; on the other hand those items to which teachers of all age groups make relatively little contribution are concerned with much more specific skills and knowledge. In some cases it may be that the class teacher herself does not contribute to these aims because specialist help is available or is thought to be necessary. This is probably true of items 68 and 49, and possibly, 41. On the other hand the fact that these items also received low rank positions when teachers were asked about their importance as 'ultimate' aims (Ashton *et al.*, 1974) suggests that, for teachers as a whole, aims that are considered important are also those to which a contribution is made; correspondingly aims that are considered unimportant are those to which little or no contribution is made. That this is so can be seen from the rank correlation coefficients between the ranking of aims by mean *importance*, and the ranking produced by each group on the basis of mean *contribution*. These coefficients are presented in Table 2.

These rank correlations are also very high and it is noticeable that they become progressively higher, the higher the age of the pupils—a characteristic to be expected when it is remembered that the 'importance' ratings were concerned with the ultimate objectives of primary education.

D

Table 2: Spearman's rank correlation coefficients between items ranked on importance and the same items ranked on contribution at four age levels

Age group	Correlation with 'importance' ranking
5-year-old	·824
7-year-old	·899
9-year-old	·907
11-year-old	·929

The Nature of the Differences Between Groups

(a) *Differences in overall level of emphasis*

The first of the differences to be investigated is the extent to which teachers of each of the four age groups give an overall response which differs from that of teachers of the other age groups. For each group a mean rating across *all* items was computed yielding 2·07, 2·11, 2·23 and 2·32 for age groups five, seven, nine and 11 respectively. Thus, it seems, teachers of 11-year-olds see themselves as contributing more, on average, to more of the aims than do teachers of five-year-olds, with teachers of seven- and nine-year-olds coming somewhere between the two.

This finding is expressed in a somewhat different way in Diagram 1. Counts were made of the numbers of items with means between 1·0 and 1·5, between 1·5 and 2·5, and between 2·5 and 3·0 for each of the four groups. The first of these categories was interpreted as, on average, 'little or no contribution', the second as a 'moderate contribution' and the third as a 'considerable contribution'. The diagram shows that teachers of five-year-olds see themselves as making a 'considerable contribution' to fewer aims than do teachers of 11-year-olds, while the latter group make a considerable or moderate contribution to more aims than does the former. There is also some suggestion of a gradation within the age ranges representing the two stages of primary education, infant and junior. At seven, a larger number of aims receive 'considerable' attention than at five, and at 11 a larger number than at nine. Each stage in primary education seems to get a base line and a target in respect of the number of aims to which a contribution is made.

(b) *Differences in the Emphasis Placed on Particular Items*

Full details of the means and standard deviations of responses for each age group appear in Appendix 2. Here we concentrate attention on a few items which show up particularly large differences among the four age groups.

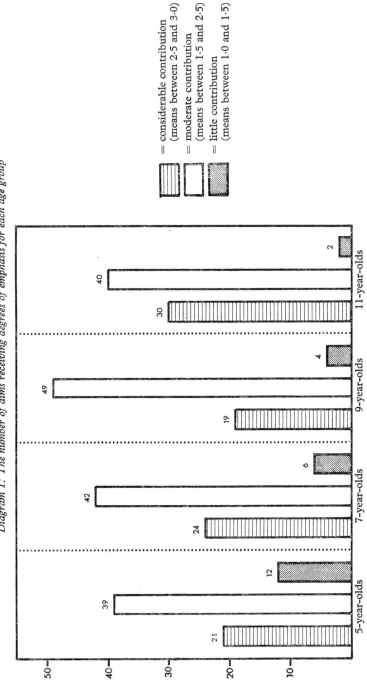

Diagram 1: The number of aims receiving degrees of emphasis for each age group

= considerable contribution
(means between 2·5 and 3·0)

= moderate contribution
(means between 1·5 and 2·5)

= little contribution
(means between 1·0 and 1·5)

5-year-olds: 21, 39, 12

7-year-olds: 24, 42, 6

9-year-olds: 19, 49, 4

11-year-olds: 30, 40, 2

Four such items are concerned with basic literary skills, namely:

56. The child should be developing the skills of acquiring knowledge and information from written material; for example summarizing, taking notes accurately, the use of libraries;

34. The child should know how to write clear and meaningful English appropriate to different formal purposes; for example, factual reports, letters, descriptive accounts;

42. The child should know the basic grammatical rules of written English;

5. The child should know the correct spelling of a basic general vocabulary.

Teachers of 11-year-olds see themselves as making a much bigger contribution to each of the above aims than do teachers of five-year-olds. Teachers of nine-year-olds make similar contributions to those made by teachers of 11-year-olds, while the biggest change in emphasis comes between five and seven for three aims (56, 34, 5), and between seven and nine for one (42).

Another item which is emphasized much more by teachers of 11-year-olds than by teachers of five-year-olds is:

63. The child should know how to play a variety of games; for example, football, skittleball, rounders.

Teachers of five- and seven-year-olds contribute relatively little to the development of such ball-game skills, while their colleagues teaching older children regard themselves as making a much larger contribution.

The child's ability to use the four rules of arithmetic (item 29) is a sixth item on which the responses of the groups differ substantially. On average, teachers of five-year-olds make a 'moderate' contribution to the teaching of number skills, while teachers of the other age groups make a more 'considerable' contribution.

For all of the items mentioned so far in this section the emphasis has increased from age five to age 11. Relatively few items produced substantially different means for the four groups, with the teachers of five-year-olds making a bigger contribution than teachers of 11-year-olds. Some significant differences of this sort do, however, emerge, and the following items constitute major examples:

30. The child should be a good mixer; he should be able to make easy social contacts with other children and adults in work and play situations;

7. The child should be an individual, developing in his own way;

54. The child should know the appropriate techniques of some arts and crafts; for example how to use paint, clay.

These three items represent aspects of education related to personal, social and aesthetic development. In each case, the emphasis is relatively high for ages five and seven, that is to say in the infant or first school, and significantly lower at ages nine and 11. Further evidence relating to a declining emphasis on these aspects of education is presented later (p. 59). Here we can just note that the English infant school is continuing its tradition of concern for the individual development of the child, while the junior school sees itself as faced with the task of changing emphasis from individual, creative, expressive work towards more intellectual activity. The junior school makes a contribution to these other aspects of education but less of a contribution than does the infant school. That, at least, is the claim of teachers in these schools, as expressed in their responses to the questionnaire.

Diagram 2: Degree of emphasis placed on six categories of aim by age group

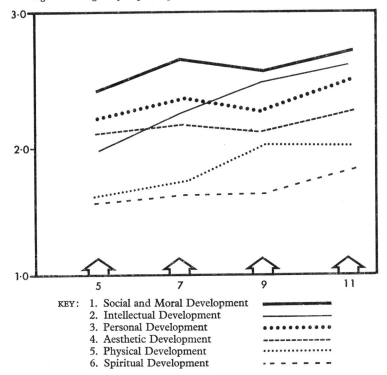

KEY: 1. Social and Moral Development ▬▬▬▬▬
      2. Intellectual Development ────────
      3. Personal Development ••••••••••
      4. Aesthetic Development ----------
      5. Physical Development ••••••••••••••••
      6. Spiritual Development - - - - - -

(c) *Differences in Emphasis by Categories of Aim*
A set of six categories was developed by teachers to contain the original
72 aims (Ashton *et al.*, op. cit.). These categories were: Social and
Moral; Intellectual; Personal; Aesthetic; Physical; Spiritual. Mean
ratings for all the items within each of these categories were computed
for each group and the results are illustrated in Diagram 2.

The Structure of Aims

So far discussion has been confined to the number of aims emphasized,
the degree of emphasis on particular aims and the nature of the emphasis
based on the original categorization of aims to social, moral, intellectual,
aesthetic, physical or spiritual development. It is possible, however,
that these original categories are not the most appropriate ones for
describing, in summary form, the categories which teachers employ. A
statistical technique known as factor analysis can be used to indicate
the categories of aims which seem to be implicit in the responses of
teachers, and which seem to constitute the best set of categories for
explaining the variation in responses made by different teachers.

The detailed results of the factor analysis are given in Appendix 3.
Below is given a description of each of the categories or factors, using
for this purpose the statements which were found to define them most
clearly. In order to distinguish the new categories from the earlier
a priori ones the term 'operational' categories will be used. The seven
operational categories were as follows:

FACTOR 1.   INTELLECTUAL: FIRST LEVEL COGNITIVE SKILLS*

Aim No.	Brief Description
71	The child should know how to think and solve problems, mathematically using basic concepts.
8	The child should be able to write legibly and know how to present his work attractively.
4	The child should know how to use mathematical techniques.
29	The child should know how to compute in the four arithmetic rules.
5	The child should know the correct spelling of a basic general vocabulary.
56	The child should be developing the skills of acquiring knowledge and information.

* For description we have drawn on Bloom's initial distinction of educational
objective as 'cognitive' and 'affective'; as having to do with the mind and the
feelings (Bloom *et al.*, 1956).

It is the repetition of 'know-how', the emphasis on basic skills and
the focus on mathematics and English which give this category its

distinctive flavour. The aims add up to more than the three Rs while
limiting themselves to a similar area of work. Reasoning, understanding
concepts and using complex skills all come in. They do so, however, as
first stage operations in intellectual development. It is for this and the
other points made that the category has been given its name, Intellectual: First Level Cognitive Skills.

FACTOR 2.   SOCIO-MORAL: FIRST LEVEL AFFECTIVE SKILLS

Aim No.	Brief Description
25	The child should be careful with and respectful of his own and other's property.
27	The child should be kind and considerate; give help to younger children.
26	The child should be able to read with understanding.
24	The child should be beginning to acquire a set of moral values.
30	The child should be a good mixer; he should be able to make easy social contacts.
28	The child should know how to engage in discussion—in a reasonable way.

This second category of aims is the complement of the first in its
emphasis on the 'how' of behaviour. Here we see simple social and
moral rules being put before the child, as well as the skills of speaking
and reading through which injunctions to behave in socially approved
and morally acceptable ways are conveyed.

FACTOR 3.   AESTHETIC-CREATIVE VERSUS INSTRUMENTAL—RULE GOVERNED

Aim No.	Brief Description
1	The child should be able to communicate his feelings through some art forms.
60	The child should be developing his inventiveness and creativity.
16	The child should have sufficient knowledge and skill to be able to engage in simple music making.
54	The child should know the appropriate techniques of some arts and crafts.
48	The child should be beginning to understand aesthetic experience.
	Versus
42	The child should know the basic grammatic rules of written English.

Here we have a category of aims which clearly has to do with aesthetic
and expressive experience, with creativity in one direction and with
following rules in the other. Aim No. 42 with its instrumental quality

is at one end of a dimension on which aims concerned with aesthetic experience in areas of expression—art, craft, music—and creativity are to be found at the other.

FACTOR 4.   SOCIO-MORAL: SECOND LEVEL AFFECTIVE SKILLS

Aim No.	Brief Description
47	The child should be enthusiastic and eager to put his best into all activities.
50	The child should be able to listen with concentration and understanding.
43	The child should know how to behave with courtesy and good manners.
38	The child should be developing the ability to control his behaviour and his emotions.
40	The child should be self confident; he should have a sense of personal adequacy.

This category of aims can be distinguished from the *Socio-Moral First Level* category by the degree of complexity of the behaviour which they incorporate. Understanding why rather than rule following or simply knowing that particular behaviour is required are characteristic of some of the aims of this category. Others call for the development of certain personal dispositions and attitudes toward what the child engages on. The achievement of the aims of this Second Level category calls for the internalization of a wide range of lesser social skills; those represented at the first level.

FACTOR 5.   SPIRITUAL: AFFECTIVE DISPOSITIONS

Aim No.	Brief Description
10	The child should be developing awareness of the spiritual aspects of prayer and worship.
6	The child should have some knowledge of the Bible and Christian beliefs.
67	The child should try to behave in accordance with the ideals of the Christian religion.
19	The child should try to behave in accordance with the ideals of his own religion.
58	The child should be generally obedient to parents, teachers.

This is clearly a Spiritual or Religious category of aims being mainly concerned with awareness and knowledge of aspects of religious life, and perhaps with the conforming behaviour for which these aims sometimes seem to call.

The intellectual skills reflected in this group of aims call for the co-ordination of a much more intricate range of subordinate skills for

FACTOR 6. INTELLECTUAL: SECOND LEVEL COGNITIVE SKILLS

Aim No.	*Brief Description*
36	The child should have some idea of modern technological developments.
54	The child should know the appropriate techniques of some arts and crafts.
35	The child should have ordered subject knowledge in, for example, history, geography.
34	The child should know how to write clear and meaningful English appropriate to different formal purposes.
37	The child should be developing a critical and discriminating attitude towards his experiences.

their achievement than would be the case for the achievement of the first category of aims identified—Intellectual: First Level Cognitive Skill. For the achievement of these Second Level aims children would need to have developed a pre-adolescent level of cognitive maturity.

FACTOR 7. PERSONAL DEVELOPMENT: SELF-ACTUALIZATION: EFFECTIVE

Aim No.	*Brief Description*
69	The child should begin to realize that he can play an important part in his own development.
9	The child should be developing the ability to make reasoned judgements and choices.
49	The child should be developing a personal appreciation of beauty.
22	The child should be developing the capacity to form a considered opinion and act upon it.
64	The child should be beginning to feel community responsibility.

This final category described as Personal Development is the most difficult to define. It represents the 'development of the child's full potential' of the Plowden Report (1967), and for that matter of the 'open' or 'progressive' view of primary education. It is also related to what Maslow has described as the 'self-actualizing individual' (1962), and is a grouping of aims which focuses on the individual child as a person in his own right. It also represents a constellation of aims which are difficult for the teacher to achieve. To bring a child to an awareness of himself, his abilities, attitudes and interests—and his responsibilities—is demanding of great skill and devotion and such aims cannot be achieved either easily or quickly. Their achievement takes time to mature, but must be begun in the primary school.

The seven categories of aim outlined above constitute a set of categories which best represent the ways in which teachers perceive the aims and the categories in relation to which this may make differences of emphasis. It is of interest to note that no category of 'Physical Development' appears: this may, however, simply result from teachers' agreement with one another about the aims of Physical Development. Alternatively, the items originally classified as 'Physical' may have resulted in responses which align them rather more with items in other categories. Thus, for example, items 2 and 41, concerned with understanding how the body works and sex education respectively, were closely related to the category *Second Level Cognitive Skills*. The item concerned with emphasizing the playing of a variety of games (63) was related to the category *First Level Cognitive Skills*.

The seven operational categories suggest that Intellectual/Cognitive Aims and Social/Moral Aims can be divided between two levels, an upper and a lower level, while the remaining three groups are more unitary. Overall, though, the impression gained from the factor analysis is that the operational categories are not very different from the *a priori* categories which the teachers developed to generate the 72 aims used initially.

Differences Between the Groups on the Operational Categories

Teachers' scores on each of the factors were computed and the results subjected to a multivariate analysis of variance.[1] The results are reported in Table 1 and a visual representation of them appears in Diagram 3. Much the same differences in emphasis on categories of aims appear as were found earlier. Both groupings of intellectual aims (cognitive 1 and 2) are given relatively little emphasis at the earliest stage and increasing emphasis at later stages. There is also a difference

Table 3: Mean factor scores for seven categories of aims for each of four age groups

	AGE GROUPS			
	Five	*Seven*	*Nine*	*Eleven*
Intellectual: Cognitive 1	—·61	·08	·32	·23
Social-Moral Affective 1	·01	·17	—·23	—·02
Aesthetic Creative Affective	·25	·12	—·19	—·20
Socio-Moral Affective 2	·06	·15	·09	·13
Spiritual Affective	—·002	—·006	·005	·003
Intellectual: Cognitive 2	—·68	—·22	·34	·61
Personal Development	—·08	—·05	—·07	—·19

Within Factor F ratios
(NDFL=3 NDF2=515)
Overall Discrimination: F ratio 21·33, p < ·001 (NDF1=21, NDF2=1462)
(NDFL=3 NDF2=515)

[1] See Appendix 4 for technical details.

in the timing of emphasis on the two intellectual categories, the first
receiving an early emphasis, the second a later one.

The relative emphasis on the Aesthetic-Creative group of aims is in
quite a different direction from the two intellectual groups. Aesthetic-
Creative aims appear to receive significantly greater emphasis at ages

Diagram 3: Differences in emphasis on each of five categories of aims based on
mean factor scores*

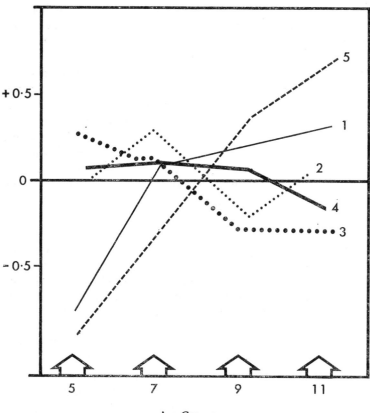

Age Groups

* No measurable difference was discernible on mean factor scores for operational Category 5 Aims: Spiritual; and Category 7 Aims: Personal Development.

KEY: 1. Intellectual: First Level Cognitive Skills.
      2. Socio-Moral: First Level Affective Skills.
      3. Aesthetic-Creative Affective Dispositions.
      4. Socio-Moral: Second Level Affective Skills.
      5. Intellectual: Second Level Cognitive Skills.

five and seven than at nine and 11. There was an earlier hint of such
(see Diagram 2) a difference in the relatively weaker emphasis on
Aesthetic-Creative aims at ages nine and 11 but it was not strong.

For the remaining categories of aims the differences in emphasis
from age to age are no more than minor fluctuations, variations on
themes within their teaching to which all primary school teachers give
equal emphasis.

Socio-moral aims remain for all groups the most firmly emphasized
and Spiritual the least. Aims concerned with Personal Development
receive their fair weight of emphasis but it is the swing in the relative
emphasis placed on Aesthetic and Intellectual aims which marks the
basic difference between the teaching which the child will receive as an
'infant' and as a 'junior' in the primary school. On to an education
grounded in social and moral purposes, concerned with each child's
individuality and his need for spiritual awareness, the infant school
will, through its emphasis on creative involvement and openness, graft
the beginnings of intellectual capability. Thereafter the junior school
will broaden this basic intellectual capability into a wide range of mental
aptitudes of the kind which fit the child to begin to understand the
complexities of the modern world, its technologies, its social forms and
its beliefs. It would seem that the price for the increased emphasis on
intellectual skills is a relatively diminished emphasis on aesthetic-
creative aims but the fall in emphasis may be slight.

At the junior stage, as was noted earlier, teachers emphasize more
strongly more aims than teachers of infants. It may be that what the
child between seven + and 11 + gains is a broadening of his education,
with intellectual aims singled out for particular emphasis. Both the
longer school day and the increasing maturity of the child allow for
this to become a practical possibility.

The differences which have been identified are not only differences
in emphasis between the two phases of primary education, they are also
different in educational style. Each phase has its own central theme in
relation to which other emphasis would seem to be subordinate, to be
the backcloth of the drama or the lesser players in the action. At the
infant stage the child's sense of purpose, of skill and ingenuity is
directed into creative pursuits. It is here that reward is given and may
be easiest to give. It is here that motivation grows and out of its growth
comes a readiness to take on other, harder tasks, less immediately
rewarding. Thus the child is prepared for the later tasks which can less
easily be seen by him as relevant. Teaching the child to enjoy school, to
trust those around him and try such intellectual tasks as learning to

read and understand number is what the first school may well be doing. It is for the junior stage to build on this its concerns for deepening the child's intellectual promise and to lay the foundations for the more complex cognitive capabilities which develop with adolescence; but underlying both stages is a concern to facilitate the child's personal development.

Concluding Comments

This study has been concerned with the aims which teachers *say* they emphasize in their teaching and has provided a broad picture of the intentions which inform teaching in the primary school. It is clear that different patterns of intention operate with different age groups but that for all age groups social and moral purposes, together with a concern for the individual development of the child, provide substantial foundations upon which these different patterns are based.

As the child moves through the cycle of primary education, he is brought into contact with an ever widening range of experiences which extend his repertoire of learning and responding, and which serve him in many contexts, both social and personal. At the start he learns to like and value learning and to adjust to the social context in which it takes place. At the end he is learning to understand the meaning of his own and other's overt behaviour, and command complex cognitiveskills.

In the way in which it emphasizes different aims at different stages, the primary school conducts a pedagogic socialization; an *educationalization*, so that the child's capacity to cope with society and his potential capacity to change his relations to it, and to take from it what he values, is enhanced (Brim and Wheeler, 1966).

Nothing in this study can be used to say that the aims which teachers emphasize are necessarily the right ones. All that can be deduced is a picture of the variation of aims over the years of primary schooling. This picture accords well with what one expects primary schools to be attempting to achieve, and for the first time offers a systematic structure for the wide variety of statements through which the intentions of primary education are communicated. The next step is to attempt to understand just how, in the daily bustle of primary school classrooms, the intentions are achieved. To match what teachers intend to achieve with how they set about realizing these intentions is to study the dynamics of teaching in the primary school—an altogether more complicated study than this one has been. If this study has set the scene for a start to be made on understanding how the primary school is successful, it will have made an appropriate contribution.

References

ASHTON, P. M., *et al*. (1974) *Aims in Primary Education*. London: Macmillan/ Schools Council.
BLOOM, B., *et al*. (1956) *Taxonomy of Educational Objectives. Handbook I: The Cognitive Domain*. London: Longman.
BRIM, O. G., and WHEELER, S. (1966) *Socialization After Childhood*. New York: Wiley.
CENTRAL ADVISORY COUNCIL (1967). *Children and their Primary Schools (Plowden Report)*. London: HMSO.
KRATHWOHL, D. R., *et al*. (1964) *Taxonomy of Educational Objectives. Handbook 2. The Affective Domain*. London: Longman.
MASLOW, A. (1962) *Toward a Psychology of Being*. Princeton, NJ: Van Nostrand.

Appendix I

List of Aims rated by Teachers

1. The child should be able to communicate his feelings through some art forms; for example, painting, music, drama, movement.

2. The child should have an understanding of how his body works.

3. The child should know how to acquire information other than by reading; for example, by asking questions, by experimenting, from watching television.

4. The child should know how to use mathematical techniques in his everyday life; for instance, estimating distances, classifying objects, using money.

5. The child should know the correct spelling of a basic general vocabulary.

6. The child should have some knowledge of the Bible and Christian beliefs.

7. The child should be an individual, developing in his own way.

8. The child should be able to write legibly and know how to present his work attractively.

9. The child should be developing the ability to make reasoned judgements and choices, based on the interpretation and evaluation of relevant information.

10. The child should be developing awareness of the spiritual aspects of prayer and worship.

11. The child should find enjoyment in some purposeful leisure time interests and activities, both on his own and with others.

12. The child should be able to read fluently and accurately at a minimum reading age of 11.

13. The child should find enjoyment in a variety of aspects of school work and gain satisfaction from his own achievements.

14. The child should have a wide general (not subject-based) knowledge of times and places beyond his immediate experience.

15. The child should know how to observe carefully, accurately and with sensitivity.

16. The child should have sufficient knowledge and skill to be able to engage in simple music making; for example, singing, percussion, home made instruments.

17. The child should be industrious, persistent and conscientious.

18. The child should be generally obedient to parents, teachers and all reasonable authority.

19. The child should try to behave in accordance with the ideals of his own religion, whether or not this is Christian.

20. The child should know how to behave appropriately in a variety of situations; for example, talking to visitors, going on outings, answering the telephone.

21. The child should know how to convey his meaning clearly and accurately through speech for a variety of purposes; for example, description, explanation, narration.

22. The child should be developing the capacity to form a considered opinion and to act upon it even if this means rejecting conventional thought and behaviour.

23. The child should know how to apply the basic principles of health, hygiene and safety.

24. The child should be beginning to acquire a set of moral values on which to base his own behaviour; for example, honesty, sincerity, personal responsibility.

25. The child should be careful with and respectful of both his own and other people's property.

26. The child should be able to read with understanding material appropriate to his age group and interests.

27. The child should be kind and considerate; he should, for example, be willing to give personal help to younger or new children, to consider the elderly, the disabled.

28. The child should know how to engage in discussion; for example, he should be able to talk about his own and others' opinions in a reasonable way.

29. The child should know how to compute in the four arithmetic

rules using his knowledge of, for instance, number, multiplication tables and different units of measurement.

30. The child should be a good mixer; he should be able to make easy social contacts with other children and adults in work and play situations.

31. The child should know those moral values, relating to people and property, which are shared by the majority of members of the society.

32. The child should know how to speak in a clear and fluent manner appropriate to different situations; for example, informal occasions with children and adults, formal occasions.

33. The child should have precise and economic body control for all ordinary physical activities including the handling of tools and equipment.

34. The child should know how to write clear and meaningful English appropriate to different formal purposes; for example, factual reports, letters, descriptive accounts.

35. The child should have ordered subject knowledge in, for example, history, geography.

36. The child should have some understanding of modern technological developments; for example, space travel, telecommunications, automation.

37. The child should be developing a critical and discriminating attitude towards his experiences; for example, of the mass media.

38. The child should be developing the ability to control his behaviour and his emotions.

39. The child should know how to write interestingly and with sensitivity.

40. The child should be self confident; he should have a sense of personal adequacy and be able to cope with his environment at an appropriate level.

41. The child should know the basic facts of sex and reproduction.

42. The child should know the basic grammatical rules of written English.

43. The child should know how to behave with courtesy and good manners both in and out of school.

44. The child should be able to maintain lasting relationships with a few close friends.

45. The child should be adaptable to changing circumstances and flexible in outlook.

46. The child should be developing a personal appreciation of beauty in some of its forms both natural and artistic.

47. The child should be enthusiastic and eager to put his best into all activities.

48. The child should be beginning to understand aesthetic experiences and should be able to talk about them; for example, looking at pictures and sculptures, listening to poetry and plays.

49. The child should be able to play a musical instrument, such as a recorder, violin, guitar.

50. The child should be able to listen with concentration and understanding.

51. The child should have a general knowledge of his local environment in some of the following aspects, historical, geographical, natural, economic, social.

52. The child should be beginning to understand his own emotions.

53. The child should be able to swim.

54. The child should know the appropriate techniques of some arts and crafts; for example, how to use paint, clay.

55. The child should have a wide vocabulary.

56. The child should be developing the skills of acquiring knowledge and information from written material; for example, summarizing, taking notes accurately, the use of libraries.

57. The child should be developing the ability to plan independent work and organize his own time.

58. The child should be happy, cheerful and well balanced.

59. The child should know what to do in emergencies; for example, fire, sickness, accident.

60. The child should be developing his inventiveness and creativity in some fields; for example, painting, music, mechanical things, poetry, movement.

61. The child should have some knowledge of the beliefs of the major world religions other than Christianity.

62. The child should know some simple scientific experimental procedures and some basic scientific concepts; for example, properties of materials, the nature and significance of changes in living things.

63. The child should know how to play a variety of games; for example, football, skittle-ball, rounders.

64. The child should be beginning to feel community responsibility; for example, he should be loyal to groups such as class and school of which he is a member and, where possible, the wider community, and willing to accept the responsibilities which membership implies.

65. The child should have a questioning attitude towards his environment.

E

66. The child should be developing tolerance; respecting and appreciating others, their feelings, views and capabilities.

67. The child should try to behave in accordance with the ideals of the Christian religion.

68. The child should be able to conduct a simple conversation in a foreign language.

69. The child should be beginning to realize that he can play an important part in his own development by, for example, recognizing his strengths and limitations and setting his own goals accordingly.

70. The child should be able to listen to and enjoy a range of music; for example, pop, folk, classical.

71. The child should know how to think and solve problems mathematically using the appropriate basic concepts of, for example, the number system and place value, shape, spatial relationships, sets, symmetry and the appropriate language.

72. The child should have a range of movement and gymnastic skills.

Appendix 2

Means and standard deviations of aims for each group

	FIVE-YEAR-OLDS		SEVEN-YEAR-OLDS		NINE-YEAR-OLDS		ELEVEN-YEAR-OLDS	
Aim	Mean	Standard Deviation	Mean	Standard Deviation	Mean	Standard Deviation	Mean	Standard Deviation
1	2·54	0·57	2·43	0·60	2·26	0·59	2·29	0·62
2	1·46	0·60	1·51	0·61	1·80	0·64	1·95	0·58
3	2·50	0·65	2·60	0·55	2·65	0·49	2·60	0·53
4	2·19	0·72	2·60	0·55	2·70	0·52	2·67	0·49
5	1·85	0·75	2·34	0·64	2·49	0·53	2·57	0·51
6	2·03	0·69	2·17	0·66	2·15	0·75	2·14	0·69
7	2·74	0·66	2·65	0·55	2·44	0·57	2·54	0·61
8	2·23	0·66	2·64	0·51	2·71	0·49	2·73	0·47
9	1·80	0·70	2·14	0·65	2·30	0·63	2·40	0·60
10	1·61	0·68	1·70	0·69	1·71	0·77	1·76	0·71
11	2·12	0·72	2·22	0·74	2·22	0·70	2·29	0·69
12	2·73	0·56	2·82	0·48	2·71	0·52	2·70	0·50
13	2·86	0·37	2·89	0·31	2·74	0·43	2·78	0·43
14	1·75	0·70	2·07	0·63	2·17	0·58	2·21	0·53
15	2·12	0·68	2·30	0·60	2·28	0·62	2·33	0·57
16	2·01	0·66	2·04	0·74	1·76	0·77	1·86	0·77
17	2·39	0·67	2·55	0·54	2·44	0·57	2·55	0·54
18	2·75	0·48	2·78	0·43	2·60	0·54	2·69	0·49
19	1·93	0·79	1·92	0·74	1·96	0·79	2·02	0·74

Aims in Primary Education

Appendix 2—*continued*

	FIVE-YEAR-OLDS		SEVEN-YEAR-OLDS		NINE-YEAR-OLDS		ELEVEN-YEAR-OLDS	
Aim	Mean	Standard Deviation	Mean	Standard Deviation	Mean	Standard Deviation	Mean	Standard Deviation
20	2·32	0·64	2·24	0·70	2·27	0·69	2·50	0·58
21	2·49	0·56	2·58	0·52	2·53	0·53	2·56	0·54
22	1·50	0·63	1·76	0·68	1·74	0·65	1·98	0·67
23	2·31	0·63	2·24	0·67	2·22	0·61	2·31	0·62
24	2·67	0·55	2·78	0·43	2·69	0·46	2·81	0·41
25	2·84	0·40	2·85	0·35	2·70	0·48	2·82	0·38
26	2·76	0·54	2·95	0·22	2·84	0·37	2·73	0·46
27	2·60	0·56	2·74	0·44	2·50	0·56	2·68	0·48
28	2·15	0·71	2·26	0·60	2·22	0·62	2·40	0·52
29	1·94	0·79	2·56	0·55	2·71	0·50	2·66	0·51
30	2·61	0·55	2·54	0·58	2·28	0·61	2·36	0·59
31	2·51	0·61	2·57	0·56	2·47	0·55	2·57	0·55
32	2·05	0·72	2·16	0·65	2·02	0·72	2·24	0·59
33	2·02	0·61	2·18	0·60	2·02	0·59	2·00	0·60
34	1·58	0·74	2·01	0·74	2·31	0·63	2·46	0·62
35	1·22	0·50	1·45	0·62	1·69	0·72	1·71	0·65
36	1·38	0·56	1·78	0·60	1·69	0·60	2·00	0·58
37	1·40	0·60	1·67	0·70	1·81	0·67	2·11	0·69
38	2·48	0·57	2·49	0·57	2·46	0·53	2·57	0·52
39	1·98	0·74	2·44	0·58	2·46	0·59	2·55	0·54
40	2·62	0·59	2·66	0·56	2·49	0·58	2·60	0·52
41	1·26	0·52	1·29	0·54	1·45	0·62	1·56	0·67
42	1·43	0·66	1·77	0·76	2·24	0·74	2·28	0·66
43	2·73	0·46	2·75	0·45	2·65	0·49	2·78	0·42
44	1·68	0·75	1·79	0·72	1·78	0·78	1·87	0·66
45	2·01	0·65	2·15	0·65	2·02	0·64	2·17	0·69
46	2·18	0·64	2·34	0·60	2·24	0·63	2·21	0·58
47	2·75	0·45	2·78	0·41	2·69	0·50	2·67	0·52
48	1·98	0·66	2·08	0·62	2·00	0·68	2·12	0·63
49	1·15	0·38	1·28	0·54	1·42	0·64	1·62	0·75
50	2·58	0·54	2·62	0·50	2·54	0·53	2·56	0·53
51	1·66	0·66	1·91	0·73	2·26	0·61	2·44	0·56
52	1·72	0·66	1·84	0·70	1·88	0·64	1·98	0·66
53	1·28	0·62	1·47	0·72	1·82	0·85	2·22	0·79
54	2·58	0·57	2·52	0·58	2·31	0·62	2·29	0·56
55	2·63	0·54	2·66	0·47	2·67	0·47	2·71	0·47
56	1·48	0·66	1·97	0·71	2·33	0·62	2·58	0·56
57	1·79	0·75	2·15	0·69	2·12	0·68	2·42	0·62
58	2·95	0·21	2·88	0·32	2·75	0·47	2·74	0·45
59	1·79	0·77	2·04	0·68	2·04	0·67	2·15	0·67
60	2·53	0·57	2·41	0·56	2·36	0·57	2·45	0·59
61	1·16	0·44	1·14	0·41	1·39	0·59	1·48	0·61
62	1·61	0·64	1·77	0·63	2·01	0·65	2·09	0·60
63	1·28	0·53	1·57	0·69	2·25	0·70	2·27	0·65
64	1·96	0·73	2·36	0·66	2·37	0·62	2·58	0·54
65	2·41	0·66	2·48	0·68	2·46	0·59	2·52	0·58
66	2·51	0·57	2·58	0·54	2·57	0·49	2·66	0·52
67	2·05	0·73	2·16	0·71	2·21	0·72	2·19	0·69

68 Aims, Influence and Change

Appendix 2—*continued*

Aim	FIVE-YEAR-OLDS Mean	Standard Deviation	SEVEN-YEAR-OLDS Mean	Standard Deviation	NINE-YEAR-OLDS Mean	Standard Deviation	ELEVEN-YEAR-OLDS Mean	Standard Deviation
68	1·05	0·24	1·07	0·29	1·18	0·48	1·27	0·55
69	1·74	0·70	1·87	0·72	1·90	0·69	2·08	0·62
70	1·83	0·67	1·89	0·65	1·75	0·69	1·91	0·67
71	2·00	0·76	2·36	0·63	2·55	0·59	2·53	0·54
72	2·01	0·61	2·21	0·70	2·19	0·69	2·08	0·60

Appendix 3

Factor analysis: Varimax loadings

	1	2	3	4	5	6	7
1		0·238	0·651				
2					0·214	0·480	0·290
3	0·397	0·253	0·220				0·389
4	0·565						
5	0·553				0·300	0·366	
6					0·743		
7			0·277			0·468	
8	0·601	0·231			0·255	0·210	
9	0·418					0·239	0·547
10					0·744		
11							0·411
12	0·341	0·267					
13	0·205	0·311	0·309		0·225		0·268
14	0·341	0·365				0·300	0·226
15	0·296	0·393					0·383
16		0·253	0·594		0·279		
17	0·294	0·438			0·344		
18		0·527			0·372		
19		0·250			0·630		
20		0·524				0·229	0·300
21		0·530					0·298
22		0·342				0·346	0·495
23		0·507					
24	0·237	0·601		0·231	0·202		
25		0·699		0·229			
26	0·308	0·605					
27		0·655		0·204			
28		0·519					0·282
29	0·559	0·365				0·344	
30		0·568	0·256				
31		0·465		0·240	0·269		

Appendix 3—*continued*

	1	2	3	4	5	6	7
32	0·451					0·215	0·254
33			0·271	0·201		0·286	
34	0·341					0·574	
35	0·217					0·566	
36						0·628	
37						0·546	0·414
38				0·526		0·237	0·208
39	0·355			0·326		0·420	
40				0·510			0·338
41						0·506	
42	0·358		−0·236	0·216		0·549	
43		0·267		0·558	0·271		
44				0·260		0·348	0·398
45				0·363			0·516
46			0·358	0·415			0·385
47				0·582			
48			0·363	0·327		0·277	0·375
49			0·267			0·488	
50		0·270		0·575			
51	0·219					0·526	
52				0·318		0·320	0·417
53						0·588	
54			0·547	0·392			
55	0·424			0·443			
56	0·497					0·503	
57	0·391			0·224		0·216	0·411
58			0·275	0·525			
59	0·205			0·214		0·350	0·239
60			0·627	0·216			0·266
61					0·264	0·457	0·223
62	0·362					0·405	
63	0·359					0·545	
64	0·355			0·215			0·479
65			0·275	0·233			0·478
66	0·225			0·343			0·428
67				0·219	0·723		
68						0·404	
69	0·275						0·573
70			0·452				0·235
71	0·620		0·210				
72	0·314		0·377				

Appendix 4

Factor scores and multivariate analysis of variance

A factor is, in a sense, a composite variable. From responses on questionnaire items (variables) can be derived the smaller number of composite variables we call factors. Inasmuch as individuals differ from one another in their responses to the original items, so do they differ from one another in their (implicit) rating of the factors (composite variable). These differences are expressed by computing, for each respondent, a score on a particular factor. Such a 'factor score' is derived from a combination of his responses to the items in the questionnaire and the loadings of the items on the factor. Factor scores are thus scores of individual respondents on factors (composite variables) just as a response to an item in a questionnaire is a 'score' on that item for the individual concerned. The only difference is that factor scores are already standardized, which means that over the whole sample the mean factor score is approximately zero and the standard deviation of factor scores approximately 1·0.

Factor scores were computed[1] for each of the 519 teachers on the basis of the Varimax factor solution. Each of these factors, is, by definition, independent of each of the others. The question that arises is whether teachers of 5-year-olds, 7-year-olds, 9-year-olds and 11-year-olds respectively, emphasize the different factors differently from the emphasis placed upon them by the other groups. To answer this question, mean factor scores were computed on each factor for each of the four groups of teachers. Although the overall mean factor score must be zero it does not necessarily follow that the mean factor score for a particular sub-group of teachers will be zero. It is likely in fact that in each case there will be differences between means of the groups; the question is whether such differences arise as a result of chance or whether they are statistically significant. An appropriate technique for asessing the extent to which a set of three or more means differ from one another significantly is analysis of variance. The result of any analysis of variance is a statistic termed an F-ratio, from which it is possible to determine the probability that the differences among the group means on a factor (or other variable) are occurring by chance alone.

Multivariate analysis of variance extends the analysis in order to answer the question:

Do the groups differ from one another not just in respect of their mean factor scores on any *one* factor, but in the *pattern* of their mean

[1] Using the computer program described in HALLWORTH, H. J., and BREBNER, A. (1965). 'A system of computer programs for use in psychology and education', British Psychological Society.

factor scores across all 7 factors at once? The F-ratio derived from a multivariate analysis of variance can be used to provide an indication of the probability that the patterns of mean factor scores on seven factors differ significantly from group to group.[1]

---

[1] cf. COOLEY, W. W., and LOHNES, P. R. (1971) *Multivariate Data Analysis.* New York: Wiley.

PART II

CURRICULUM CHANGE

Primary School Teachers' Perceptions of Discovery Learning

C. Richards (Worcester College of Education)

Introduction and Rationale

'Defensible educational thought must take account of four common-places of *equal* rank—the learner, the teacher, the milieu and the subject matter ... Despite the educational bandwagons which bear witness to the contrary, neither child nor society nor subject matter nor teachers is the proper centre of curriculum' (Schwab, 1973). The 'polyfocal' complexity of curriculum is compounded by the fact that these four commonplaces can be viewed on at least two levels. They can be discussed in terms of the interrelationships and interconnections which *ought* to exist among them (Taylor's 'intentional curriculum', 1974) or in terms of the *actual* interconnections which exist at any particular time (the 'operational curriculum').

In English primary education most recent thinking has concentrated on the first commonplace and its implications for the 'intentional curriculum'. Proposals for effecting change in schools have been the subject of considerable debate but these have rested on largely un-examined assertions about present practice. In fact, little systematic is known about what is happening in primary school classrooms. Our present knowledge of the operational curriculum is heavily based on impressionistic data with its anecdotes, brief accounts and hurried observations. In the literature, 'what is' has been neglected in favour of 'what might be' (Richards, 1974).

The research reported here focused on one aspect of the operational curriculum of the primary school in an attempt to clarify part of current practice. Discovery learning was chosen because it appeared to embody many of the basic assumptions of the more 'open' approach to primary education summarized by Barth (1969) and increasingly prominent in

75

the English educational literature since the Hadow Report of 1931. In terms of the organizational model suggested by Schon (1971), discovery learning appeared to be a central element in the 'theory' of the child-centred primary school. As such it seemed to have implications for the 'social structure' of the school and for the latter's 'soft technology'— for the techniques and programmes practised by its members. Its clarification was thus considered important in understanding the on-going reality of primary school teaching.

Specifically the research attempted to identify those learning situations which primary school teachers recognized as involving discovery learning and to relate these to discovery learning as described in research and other literature. It ascertained teachers' views as to the outcomes of discovery learning and it explored in a preliminary way teachers' perceptions of the scope of discovery learning in relation to the curriculum as a whole (Richards, 1973b). The research was based on the premise that 'it is the perception, not the reality, which is crucial in determining behaviour' (Rogers, quoted in HARGREAVE[1], D., 1972, p. 56): that the world as believed is the world as acted upon. The research assumed that how teachers perceived discovery learning situations determined in part how they reacted in the everyday trans-actions which made up the operational curriculum: that, for example, their perceptions affected the types of situations they set up, the kinds of learning they encouraged and the types of teaching procedure they employed. By means of this research it was hoped to get closer to the reality of the operational curriculum despite the latter's complexity and elusiveness. The research, however, did not claim to be in any way definitive or exhaustive of discovery learning in the primary school classroom.

Scope and Method

To explore the nature and structure of teachers' perceptions of discovery learning a questionnaire was drawn up and administered to a sample of 180 teachers. It did not prove possible within the confines of the research to supplement the questionnaire by classroom observation in selected schools.

The questionnaire consisted of six sections, the first of which was concerned with biographical details of the respondents. The second was concerned with teachers' perceptions of the general purposes of primary education, since these were believed to affect the teacher's perceptions of teaching-learning strategies and in turn to influence their handling of the operational curriculum. Teachers were asked to rate the eight broad purposes of primary education originally drawn up by Taylor *et al.* (1974). They had to select those they considered to be the two most important and the two least important.

The third section was designed to explore the nature of learning situations which teachers perceived to be cases of discovery learning. It was hoped to pinpoint paradigm cases and to explore the area of uncertainty surrounding the notion of 'discovery'. An attempt was made to capture something of the 'flavour' of the classroom by describing a large number of learning situations in the form of vignettes, each providing enough cues to enable teachers to decide whether or not discovery learning was taking place. In composing the vignettes examples were drawn from the researcher's own teaching experience and from accounts of learning situations in recent publications, especially the *British Primary Schools Today* series (1971, 1972). A group of teachers assessed the range of learning strategies covered in the vignettes by plotting the latter on a grid consisting of a child-directed/teacher-directed axis and a discovery-reception axis (Ausubel, 1968). The final list of 33 vignettes incorporated a wide range of learning situations from all the primary age-groups from five to 11 and all the major knowledge areas except religious education (see Appendix 1). When completing the questionnaire, respondents read through each vignette, asked themselves 'Is this a case of discovery learning?' and responded on a five-point Likert-type scale ranging from 'definitely' discovery learning, through 'probably', 'not sure', 'probably not' to 'definitely not' discovery learning.

A fourth section of the questionnaire examined what teachers saw as the major outcomes of discovery learning. A list of possible outcomes was drawn up, incorporating the hypotheses of Bruner (1961), Wittrock (1966), Morrisett (1966), Biggs (1966), Szabo (1967), Kersh (1965) and the Plowden Committee (1967). Other items focused on the classroom and on the claims made for child-centred education (of which discovery learning was seen as one component). Seventeen items were included in this section and a rubric asked respondents to rate on a five-point scale the extent to which they agreed with each of the items. Following discussions with a pilot group of teachers the rubric was modified to indicate that the statements applied to 'children of average and above average ability'.

A fifth section of the questionnaire, which will not be discussed in detail in this paper, set out to examine some of the practicalities involved in the successful institutionalization of discovery learning. Forty-six factors possibly promoting this approach were drawn up and teachers asked to indicate those they considered of crucial importance in promoting discovery.

The final section was a short one, designed to explore in a general way the scope of discovery learning in relation to the areas of the primary school curriculum. Five summary statements were drawn up and teachers asked to put a cross by the *one* statement with which they were most in agreement.

The Sample

The research was an exploratory study, seeking what might be relevant or significant in a relatively uncharted area. It did not seek to set up hypotheses nor to generalize from the sample of teachers to the teaching population as a whole. As an exploratory study it did not necessitate the use of a representative sample of schools or teachers. The 15 schools forming the research sample were chosen, not for their representative nature but simply because their staffs were willing to participate in the study.

There were three infant, four junior and eight junior and infant schools from four local authorities, three of which covered wholly urban areas. Five of the schools were of open-plan design and all of these had been in existence for less than four years at the time of the study. One school was particularly well-known in its authority as a pioneer of new teaching methods, and only two schools had a high proportion of immigrants (in both cases over 40 per cent).

Of 180 questionnaires distributed, 140 were returned completed—a response rate of 77·8 per cent. Fifty-two per cent of respondents had been teaching less than six years, three-quarters were women and two-thirds were married. Only 30 per cent of the sample had been teaching for more than 10 years. The sample was distributed six to four between teachers holding posts of responsibility or seniority and assistant teachers. There was a fairly even spread of respondents teaching each of the age-groups five to seven, seven to nine and nine to 11. All the findings which emerged were strictly applicable only to those 140 teeachers. However, it could be argued that in most respects they were reasonably representative of primary school teachers in general.

Teachers' Perceptions of the Purposes of Primary Education

The respondents' perceptions of the relative emphasis to be given to eight purposes of primary education threw light on the operational curriculum in the sample schools and allowed comparisons to be made between respondents' views and those of a group of teachers from 12 'typical' urban primary schools who completed an identical section in an earlier study (Taylor *et al.*, 1974).

The responses from sample schools are summarized in Table 1. Of the eight purposes, only intellectual development was considered by over half the sample to be one of the two most important purposes. Only 2·9 per cent of respondents regarded it as of least importance, but some 40 per cent did not place it as one of their major emphases. Just under half the teachers were agreed that physical and emotional development were among the two most important purposes, with the development of social awareness being similarly rated by 30 per cent. The greatest degree of consensus (84·3 per cent) was on rating spiritual development as one of the two least important emphases: no other purpose was so rated by over half the sample. The remaining purposes fell into an intermediate category.

Table 1: Percentage of the sample judging each of eight purposes of primary education as one of the two most important, one of the two least important or neither

Purpose	% Most Important	% Neither	% Least Important
Spiritual development	2·1	13·6	84·3
Aesthetic awareness	7·9	64·3	27·9
Intellectual development	60·0	37·1	2·9
Practical skills	21·4	49·3	29·3
Physical and emotional development	44·3	45·7	10·0
Preparation for secondary education	20·0	54·3	25·7
Moral awareness	10·0	81·4	8·6
Social awareness	30·0	67·1	2·9

An attempt was made to relate perceptions of purposes to the biographical characteristics of respondents using Goodman and Kruskal's G as a measure of association (1954, 1959, 1964). Few associations emerged as statistically significant at the five per cent level or above. Both 'status within the school' and 'length of teaching experience' were quite clearly related to ratings of spiritual development at the one per cent level. More experienced teachers, who were generally in more senior positions, placed significantly greater emphasis on spiritual development than their more junior colleagues. This might have been due to the climate of opinion during their upbringing or professional training and to their closer involvement with school assemblies. In Taylor's sample 'age-group being taught' was significantly related to each of the eight purposes but no such significant relationships appeared in the present study. However, a different picture emerged when a combination of 'age group being taught' and 'type of school' was considered. Compared with infant teachers in both infant and junior and infant schools, junior teachers placed significantly ($p > 0.05$) more emphasis on moral awareness and on physical and emotional development. Perhaps moral education was viewed as implicit in the infant classroom whereas junior teachers felt it necessary to engage in more definite moral education. Junior teachers' emphasis on physical and emotional development was somewhat unexpected and possibly due to the fact that one of the junior schools and one of the junior departments were particularly noted for their work in physical education.

As judged by responses to the second part of the questionnaire, the operational curriculum of the sample schools was one in which intellectual development was the central, but not exclusive, concern. Teachers were anxious that children should learn how to learn, should come to value learning for its own sake and should acquire a body of knowledge and skills, but they wanted these to take place alongside the fostering of physical and emotional development and the establishment of good personal relationships based on social awareness and social skills. The respondents were far from being anti-intellectual child-minders. Their perceptions of discovery learning situations and their assessment of the outcomes of discovery were informed by a marked emphasis on children's cognitive development as a major focus of the primary school curriculum.

Compared with Taylor's sample of teachers from 'typical' urban primary schools, the present respondents placed rather more emphasis on intellectual development and physical and emotional development as opposed to social awareness. Their ratings of aesthetic and spiritual development were similar to those of Taylor's sample and they consigned similar purposes to intermediate status. There was thus a fairly close correspondence between the perceptions of the two groups. This lends weight to the contention that the group of 140 respondents were fairly typical of primary school teachers in general.

Teachers' Perceptions of Classroom Learning Situations

In a primary school classroom the complex interaction of teacher, child and curriculum varies in kind, scope, pace and intensity throughout the school day. During the course of a term many different kinds of teacher-child transactions take place, many different learning situations are created and many different learning contexts arise—often unplanned in advance by either teacher or child. Which of these learning situations or contexts do primary school teachers characterize as being cases of discovery learning?

To help answer this question, an analysis was made of the sample's responses to the 33 vignettes of classroom learning situations which made up the third section of the questionnaire. Teachers were asked to rate vignettes on a scale from five ('definitely discovery learning') to one ('definitely not discovery learning'). Mean scores and standard deviations were calculated and the learning situations arranged in rank order. The cut-off points separating highly rated items, intermediate ratings and lowest mean ratings were arbitrary, though in each case the separation was marked by a sizeable gap between the scores of successive items.

(1) *Highly rated items*
Items with very high mean ratings (over 4·0) were the cases which primary school teachers regarded as definitely or very probably cases of discovery learning.

These vignettes were:

8. As part of a topic on 'fire' which he had chosen himself, John (10) set up a number of his own experiments to see the relative burning time of different types of matches. He recorded his results in his 'fire' booklet. (Mean rating = 4·59).

6. The teacher is trying to teach Ian (10) how to measure areas. She asks him to draw rectangles of various sizes on squared paper, to count the number of square centimetres inside each rectangle and to write that figure down as the area. Ian says he has found a quick way of finding the area of a rectangle. 'You just times how long it is by how wide it is, Miss'. (Mean rating = 4·58).

5. The gift of a precision geometry set inspired Scott (nine) to experiment with drawing circles, patterns and regular polygons. In the process he taught himself some geometry. (Mean rating = 4·51).

33. Alan (11) described to the class the experiment he had just completed. At the teacher's suggestion but using his own particular methods he had compared the ways in which different materials dried. His recorded results included drying curves for each material and calculations of the water content. (Mean rating = 4·48).

7. Julie (11) wanted to test the strength of various threads. After a great deal of discussion with her teacher she designed some apparatus to compare and measure strengths. She found that a greater breaking force was required to snap string than was required to break fuse wire, cotton or wool. (Mean rating = 4·41).

F

19. Simon (11) was accustomed to improvizing, using Orff-type instruments. He wanted to invent a piece of 'Chinese music' to fit into a project and after experimenting he found a scale which he described as 'spooky'. (Mean rating = 4·36).

28. The teacher asked her class how many different ways they could move. Joan (five) found three different ways; Peter found four ways. (Mean rating = 4·17).

1. At the teacher's initial suggestion, Jimmy (nine) decided to measure the speeds recorded for snails of different sizes. When he had done this using his own methods, he wrote 'I think that size doesn't have anything to do with the speed of snails'. (Mean rating = 4·05).

The extent of teachers' general agreement as to the rating of those eight items was gauged by examining the item standard deviations. Only in one case did the standard deviation reach 1·00 and only two other items had standard deviations exceeding 0·85. The frequency distribution of responses for each of the items gave the same picture. Although a high level of teacher agreement did exist, it was noteworthy that even in the cases of the two items with the highest mean ratings there were still some teachers (four in one case, seven in the other) who considered that the situations were *not* cases of discovery learning.

The teachers saw discovery learning as characterizing a range of learning situations in a variety of curriculum areas. Their perceptions were not congruent with such theorists as Foster (1972) and Marsh (1970 and 1973) who appeared to equate discovery learning with informal learning. The teachers disagreed with Bantock (1969) that finding out for oneself from books constituted a mode of discovery learning. Getting the right answer to a problem on a workcard, painting a picture, making a model or playing a piece of music did not feature in their perceptions as cases of discovery, even when the activities were undertaken at the child's own initiative and pursued in an independent way. Discovery learning and independent learning were clearly differentiated.

There did appear to be a common core underlying all eight highly rated items, though this was difficult to articulate fully. In each case the child was an active participant faced with a problem: 'Do larger snails move faster?' 'In how many ways can I move?' 'Is there a quick way of finding areas of rectangles?' In none of the cases was the problem solved by the child following strict instructions or a standard procedure. The child resolved the problem in his own (non-standard) way by exploring the situation and inferring a relationship or establishing a satisfactory pattern of cognition.

Apart from this common core the eight learning situations displayed considerable diversity. For example, the three most highly rated items constituted very different types of learning situation. The first was a problem-solving situation where the child sought an answer to a clearly defined problem and, unaided, devised his own methods for reaching a conclusion. The second situation was teacher-initiated and very highly teacher-directed, with the child being left to make the final inference himself. In almost complete contrast the third item involved open-ended exploration on the child's part with no clearly defined end in view and no teacher guidance. The multi-dimensionality of the learning situations covered by the eight items is illustrated in Table 2. In compiling this table, four dimensions of learning situations (Richards, 1973a) were combined with a fifth—a child-initiated/teacher-initiated dimension. Each of the items was characterized tentatively according to its position on each of those dimensions. The lack of any recurrent patterns across the dimensions revealed the variety of contexts in which the teachers perceived that discovery learning could occur.

Table 2: The eight most highly rated items and five dimensions of learning situations

Item No.	Dimensions				
	A	B	C	D	E
8	Planned	Child-i.	Autonomous	Concrete	Closed
6	Planned	Teacher-i.	Directed	Symbolic	Closed
5	Accidental	Child-i.	Autonomous	Symbolic	Open
33	Planned	Teacher-i.	Autonomous	Concrete	Closed(?)
7	Planned	Child-i.	Directed	Concrete	Closed
19	Planned	Child-i.	Autonomous	Concrete	Open
28	Planned	Teacher-i.	Autonomous	Concrete	Open
1	Planned	Teacher-i.	Autonomous	Concrete	Closed

A: Planned . . . Accidental activities
B: Child-initiated . . . Teacher-initiated activities
C: Autonomous . . . Directed activities
D: Use of Concrete . . . Symbolic materials
E: Open-ended . . . Closed activities

The teachers' perceptions did not fall neatly into the categories proposed by educational writers. For example, Dearden's three models of discovery learning (1967) did not adequately characterize those diverse learning contexts, nor did Biggs' typology of discovery learning (1971). Dearden's later typology of teaching strategies (1973) also failed to match up to the diversity of teachers' perceptions. Some of the eight items could not be placed within his five types, one of which (type C) was not even regarded by the respondents as a probable mode of discovery learning. Likewise, Morine's classification of discovery modes (1969) was inadequate: the 'transductive mode' (i.e. learning involving artistic methods of inquiry) was not seen as a clear mode of discovery by the majority of teachers.

The great diversity of situations characterized as discovery learning highlighted the inadequacy of the 'guided discovery—autonomous discovery' dichotomy appearing in research literature (Kersh and Wittrock, 1962). Not only was it inadequate but the dichotomy failed to do justice to the richness of classroom learning contexts revealed by the eight items. Whereas to American researchers—Worthen (1968) and Anastasiouw *et al.* (1970), for instance—discovery learning involved children working in formal classroom settings and inferring generalizations from examples in workbooks, English teachers seemed to construe it as a far richer, more diverse method of teaching and learning involving exploration, experimentation and physical activity.

Lastly it needs to be stressed that the sample of teachers did not restrict discovery learning to any particular age-group or area of the curriculum. It was seen as applicable to five-year-olds as much as to 11-year-olds. Mathematics and science were well represented among the highest ratings but music and PE each had an item with a mean rating over 4·00. If items with ratings of over 3·40 were included as probable cases of discovery learning, then social studies and language featured too.

(2) *Intermediate ratings*

Twelve items with mean ratings between 3·50 and 2·50 fell into an intermediate category. The respondents were uncertain as to whether or not these situations could be characterized as discovery learning. Of the 12, five could be classified as aesthetic activities and three as activities concerned with reference work of some kind.

(*a*) *Aesthetic activities:* In all five aestheic items children were engaged in 'creative' activities: making models, composing poems, making pieces of embroidery, producing patterns with shells. The mean standard deviation for those creative items was 1·20, above that for aesthetic items taken as a whole (1·10). This uncertainty as to the relationship of 'creative' items to discovery learning was reflected in the frequency distribution of responses. These indicated that a considerable number of respondents conflated the notions of discovery and creativity. This was not surprising since 'creativity is one of the vaguest, most ambiguous and most confused terms in psychology and education today' (Ausubel, 1968). Further research is needed to explore fully and clearly teachers' perceptions of the relationship between creativity and discovery learning.

(b) *Reference work items:* Bantock (1969), Dearden (1973) and Foster (1972) all regarded the acquisition of information from reference books as an example of discovery learning, but responses to three 'reference work' items revealed that teachers were very uncertain of this. The mean standard deviation for the items was 1·32—far higher than the mean standard deviation for the non-aesthetic items taken as a whole (1·05). Two out of the three reference work items were concerned with project work, as was another item which also fell into the intermediate category. The teachers were obviously uncertain as to the distinction project work and discovery learning, with some regarding them as synonymous and others differentiating clearly between them. Their uncertainty probably reflected the child-centred nature of both types of activity, with discovery learning being a more recent emphasis and project work being somewhat 'dated'.

(3) *Lowest mean ratings*
Five items with mean ratings below 2·00 were considered by teachers as almost certainly *not* cases of discovery learning. These were:

23. After a TV programme on cave paintings a teacher got David (eight) to paint a picture on a piece of slate. (Mean rating = 1·70).
25. In teaching Barbara the recorder the teacher plays the first phrase of 'London's burning' while Barbara (nine) fingers the notes without actual playing. Then she in turn plays the phrase the teacher has played. In this way she comes to learn the whole of 'London's burning'. (Mean rating = 1·62).
18. By showing her some marionettes he had made himself, a teacher described to Pat how fashions changed during Tudor and Stuart times. Pat (nine) drew pictures to illustrate these changes. (Mean rating = 1·61).
24. In a craftwork lesson Peter (11) made a paper sculpture by following the teacher's verbal instructions one step at a time. (Mean rating = 1·39).
11. A teacher asks Bill (10) if he can see around corners or hear around corners. After a discussion the teacher tells Bill that light cannot travel around corners but sound can. (Mean rating = 1·36).

For each item the standard deviation was relatively low, indicating a high degree of teacher agreement as to its placing. The curriculum areas covered by the items were music, art, social studies, craftwork and science. It was noteworthy that science and music (and to some extent social studies) were curriculum areas where discovery learning was perceived to occur in certain circumstances. Respondents were clearly discriminating *within* curriculum areas as to whether or not discovery learning was taking place. In all the items the teacher took the initiative and the child passively received instructions or followed standard procedures. The aesthetic items were marked by an absence of creative responses, while the other items were aptly characterized by Ausubel's term, 'reception learning'.

Ratings of Learning Situations and Biographical Variables

The relationship between the teachers' judgements of the vignettes and selected biographical variables such as length of teaching experience, age-group being taught and status of respondents showed overall very little difference of emphasis in relation to these variables. Those respondents with longer teaching experience and higher status rated one 'project' item significantly more highly as a case of discovery learning than their more junior colleagues ($p < \cdot 05$). A similar position obtained with respect to a second project item, though in that case the value needed for significance was not quite reached. In both those cases the more experienced teachers were perhaps tending to equate discovery learning with the project approach, since the latter was probably regarded as an important aspect of child-centred education when they were receiving their professional training. Teachers of older children tended to view an example of 'Socratic questioning' (Dearden's type E, 1973) as a case of discovery learning ($p < \cdot 05$), whilst teachers of younger children rated two other items more highly, one involving pattern-making with shells and the other concerned with identifying similarities and differences in words ($p < \cdot 05$ and $< \cdot 05$ respectively). Those differences in emphasis probably reflected the different kinds of learning contexts set up in junior and infant classrooms. Simple experiences with shells and letters were the essence of infant teaching, whilst the teaching of older children was more concerned with structured experience, often of a directed kind.

Structure of Teachers' Perceptions of Learning Situations

During the design stage of the questionnaire the vignettes of learning situations were drawn up in relation to several *a priori* dimensions. These were discovery-reception, teacher-directed/child-directed, creative/non-creative, and teacher-initiated/child-initiated. The structure was deliberately imposed in order to generate a range of style of classroom learning from which teachers were to identify discovery learning. However, this imposed structure might not have corresponded to the actual structure implicit in teachers' responses. The technique of factor analysis was therefore used to explore the structure of teachers' perceptions in relation to the learning situations of the vignettes. After the 33 items had been intercorrelated, a factor analysis was carried out by the Varimax method to yield a simple structure. Six significant factors were extracted accounting for 48 per cent of the total variance. These were:

Factor 1: Instruction
This was termed 'instruction' since all the items with high loadings (i.e. over 0·4) involved a large measure of teacher direction and corresponding pupil passivity. In these items the teachers initiated the activities, directed them and controlled their pace. The pupils' learning was predominantly reception learning. In none of the items did children explore situations for themselves or find patterns and relationships. Factor 1 contributed 12·59 per cent of the variance.

Factor 2: Creative v. Non-creative: composition
Although a creative/non-creative dimension was built into the list of learning situations, the respondents seemed to discriminate between two facets of creativity, which are encapsulated in factors 2 and 4. Factor 2 was a bipolar factor accounting for 8·34 per cent of the variance. It proved very difficult to find a clear short-hand description of the factor, hence its rather uninformative title. Running through all the high loadings on this factor was a clear aesthetic element concerned with writing and making models. It could perhaps be termed 'composition'. Two items were concerned with composing poetry; two were concerned with making model boats and flying balloons. In each of these the initial impetus came from the child and it was the child who was responsible for conducting the activity, though with teacher-guidance in some cases.

Factor 3: Project/Topic work
This factor accounted for 7·12 per cent of the variance but corresponded to none of the *a priori* dimensions. The item with the highest loading on the factor made explicit reference to a 'topic', whilst two others were specifically concerned with 'project' activities. Project work involving a central theme was seen to involve experiments, assignments and reference work.

Factor 4: Creative v. Non-creative: design
This factor accounted for 7·33 per cent of the variance and like factor 2 was concerned with creative activities. However, these two factors had no common items with loadings over 0·3 and therefore different facets of creativity seemed to be involved. Although this was difficult to pin-point exactly, the items loaded highly seemed to involve children searching for and making patterns. It could perhaps be termed a 'design' factor.

Factor 5: Teacher-initiated, discovery learning
This accounted for 6·96 per cent of the variance and combined two elements which were part of the imposed structure. In each item with high loadings, the teacher initiated a line of enquiry either in person or through the medium of an assignment card. Once the activity was under way, the child was free to complete it for himself through inferring some pattern or relationship.

Factor 6: Accidental v. planned discovery learning
This factor which accounted for 5·69 per cent of the variance did not correspond to any of the *a priori* dimensions, though it did appear in the author's paper on discovery learning (Richards, 1973a). The factor contrasted those situations planned in advance which led to discovery and those where discovery learning took place accidentally.

To summarize, the ratings of the 33 vignettes were intercorrelated in such a way that six factors could be held to represent about half the differences of ratings by the sample of 140 teachers. They perceived discovery learning as complex, multi-faceted and of wide application, and clearly contrasted it with instruction or reception learning.

Classroom learning situations were perceived to be very complex. In contrast to this perceived complexity, the dichotomies commonly employed in research literature seem very inadequate. Discovery learning cannot be regarded simple as 'guided' or 'autonomous', nor can it be compared simply with 'rule' learning. Means have to be found of accommodating within empirical research the multi-dimensionality of discovery learning as revealed in this analysis of teachers' perceptions of learning situations.

Teachers' Perceptions of the Outcomes of Discovery Learning
As with many aspects of education, the results of discovery learning are far from clear and very much the subject of dispute. Bantock (1969), Ausubel (1963, 1968), Froome (1970, 1973) and others are sceptical of

many of the claims made for it, whilst Bruner (1961, 1966), Hendrix (1961), Suchman (1964) and Biggs (1965) view it as wide-ranging in its effects. The fourth section of the questionnaire tried to elicit primary teachers' views of the outcomes of discovery learning with average and above average children by asking them to indicate on a five-point Likert-type scale the extent of their agreement with each of 17 statements. (See Appendix 2.)

Table 3 shows the mean scores of the items in rank order. Although there was an absence of very high ratings (i.e. means over 4·50), all 17 items had means over 3·00. Only three items had mean scores under 3·50, which was chosen as the cut-off point between neutral ratings and ratings expressing agreement with the outcomes. Clearly the respondents had positive attitudes towards discovery learning as a means of bringing about certain desired results in children's attitudes and learning. The teachers' general level of agreement to judge by the standard deviation of the items was good. Only in one case (item 2) did the standard deviation exceed 1·00.

Item 3: 'Discovery learning results in children remembering experiences and their significance more readily' stood out as the learning outcome most widely attributed to discovery learning by the sample. It was the only item where the number of respondents assigning a score of five exceeded those assigning four; only two teachers disagreed with it by rating it one or two. The promotion of children's independence and of learning by experience were also very highly rated, with very few rejections. Other important outcomes were seen to be the development of a questioning attitude, the encouragement of a measure of responsibility and the promotion of communication. In all, less than 10 per cent of the respondents disagreed with items 3, 5, 17, 15, 14, 9, 12, 13 and 10, though there were various numbers in the 'neither agree nor disagree' category.

Towards the bottom of the rank order, items 8, 11, 2, 1 and 6 were rejected by over 12 per cent of the sample, but the absence of many outright rejections (i.e. scores of one) was noteworthy. Among the five items with the lowest rating were those related to knowledge and concept acquisition. Here perhaps the less 'progressive' teachers took their stand. Though in general not opposed to discovery learning as a way of promoting independence, learning from experience, questioning attitudes and the recall of experience, they were less willing to concede its importance in transmitting knowledge or aiding concept formation. In the case of both those items, 40 or more respondents had scores in the 'uncertain' category. It seemed that a sizeable minority of teachers

Table 3: Outcomes of discovery learning: views of teachers and educationalists

Outcomes	T's Mean Ratings	Supporters	Opponents
3 Remembering experiences	4·43	Plowden (1967) Bruner (1961)	Friedlander (1965)
5 Independence	4·14	Suchman (1961, 64) Cambridge Conference (1963)	Friedlander (1965)
17 Learning from experience	4·14	Ash (1965) Walters (1965) Isaacs (1960)	
7 Questioning attitude	4·04	Szabo (1967)	
15 Responsibility	3·97	Ash (1965) Walters (1965) Isaacs (1960)	
14 Communication	3·83	Biggs (1966) Boarder (1964)	
9 New Perspectives	3·73	Isaacs (1960)	
12 Informal relationships	3·73	*	
13 Co-operation	3·70	*	
4 Interest in learning	3·66	Morrisett (1966) Bruner (1961) Richards, R. (1973) Cambridge Conference (1963) Suchman (1961, 64)	Kersh (1964) Dearden (1967)
16 Needs and interests	3·65	Ash (1965) Walters (1965)	
10 Application of skills and principles	3·58	Morrisett (1966) Bruner (1961) Plowden (1967) Bantock (1969)	Ausubel (1968) Gagné (1966) Dearden (1967)
6 Self-confidence	3·56	Morrisett (1966) Suchman (1964) Cambridge Conference (1963)	Ausubel (1968)
1 Knowledge acquisition	3·56	Cambridge Conference (1963) Bruner (1961)	Ausubel (1968) Bantock (1969) Dearden (1968)
2 Concept acquisition	3·36	Suchman (1964)	Ausubel (1968) Friedlander (1965)
11 Positive attitudes to school	3·14	*	
8 Flexible citizens	3·06	Plowden (1967)	

* These items were drawn up by the researcher and not based on passages in the literature.

were unconvinced by the claims that discovery learning promotes concept acquisition and leads to children acquiring a body of useful knowledge. The promotion of positive attitudes towards school, the development of adaptable future citizens and the development of children's self-confidence were also queried as clear outcomes of discovery learning.

During the data analysis stage of the research an attempt was made to relate respondents' ratings of outcomes to biographical variables and to ratings of the purposes of primary education. Contingency tables were drawn up and G values obtained. Within the sample there was very little difference of emphasis in relation to selected biographical variables. Length of teaching experience was not related to any significant differences in perceived outcomes. This was surprising in view of Ashton's findings (1972) that more experienced teachers tended to be more traditional in outlook than their less experienced colleagues. Teachers of younger children were differentiated from teachers of older children in relation to two perceived outcomes. To a far greater extent than junior teachers, infant teachers agreed that discovery learning leads to children learning from their own experiences in both school and out-of-school contexts (p < ·001). They also perceived discovery learning as more likely to develop children's independence of thought and action (p < ·05). Both these findings supported the widely-held view that infant teachers tend to be more 'child-centred' than junior teachers and presumably more receptive to discovery as an approach to learning. Somewhat surprisingly, teachers in junior schools agreed more strongly that discovery learning promotes more positive attitudes to school than did teachers in infant schools (p < ·05). Perhaps infant teachers presupposed a positive attitude on the part of the young child in school, whilst junior teachers were more conscious that various methods of teaching could influence a child's attitude to school, especially as he approached adolescence.

There were no significant relationships between the respondents' ratings of outcome and their ratings of intellectual, physical and emotional, and social development. However, those stressing spiritual development were more likely to disagree with the claim that discovery learning promotes the child's independence of thought and action (p < ·01). This was in line with Ashton's (*op. cit.*) findings that those stressing spiritual development tended to opt for a traditional role. Those stressing aesthetic development (who tended to be junior teachers) were less likely to agree that discovery learning results in children applying skills and principles in new contexts (p < ·05). Significant relationships at the five per cent level also emerged between high ratings on moral awareness and agreement that discovery learning promotes knowledge acquisition and co-operation with others. One final positive relationship was between a stress on practical skills and agreement that discovery learning leads to the acquisition of a body of useful knowledge ($p < \cdot05$).

In Table 3 the views of the respondents are related to those of some educational writers and theorists. Judging from their responses the teachers did not wholeheartedly support Bruner's claim that discovery learning results in intellectual potency, intrinsic motivation, conservation of memory and the learning of the heuristics of discovery (1961). They agreed that it promoted the recall of experiences and they gave a fair measure of support to intrinsic motivation as an outcome. However, they shared some of Ausubel's (1968) and Friedlander's (1965) reservations about the efficacy of discovery as a means of promoting concept acquisition and the learning of subject matter. They supported the Plowden Report's (1967) contention that discovery learning intensifies children's experience but were less agreed that it increases the probability of effective transfer of learning. Nor did they relate the everyday learning of their pupils to the future life they would lead, as did the Plowden Committee. Compared with some educationists, such as Biggs (1965) and Suchman (1964), the teachers were more moderate and discriminating in their perception of outcomes. They appeared to be sceptical about some of the 'grandios' claims made for discovery learning (Brown, 1971) but clearly saw it as important in promoting certain outcomes, largely non-cognitive in nature.

The Scope of Discovery Learning
The fourth section of the questionnaire attempted to assess the perceived value of discovery learning across the curriculum by asking teachers to endorse one statement out of five outlining the scope of discovery learning. Table 4 reveals that the respondents saw discovery as valuable in most areas of the curriculum: very few indeed confined it to only one or two areas. Discovery learning seemed an established element in the 'theory' and 'technology' of the sample primary schools studied. However, the degree to which it was valuable in various curriculum areas and its scope and value compared with other techniques of teaching and learning were not examined.

Conclusion
The research reported here was concerned with one small part of the operational curriculum of the primary school. Its focus was on the classroom as it 'is' rather than on the visionary classroom of 'should be' or 'might become'. The teachers in the sample perceived discovery

Table 4: Perceived scope of discovery learning

Item	No. of Responses	Percentage
D.1. is valuable across the whole primary school curriculum	35	25·0
D.2. is valuable in most areas of the primary school curriculum	48	34·3
D.3. is valuable in some areas of the primary school curriculum but by no means all	35	39·3
D.4. is valuable in a few areas of the primary school curriculum	2	1·4
D.5. isn't valuable in any area of the primary school curriculum	0	0·0

learning to be an important component of the curriculum, as they transacted it with pupils. Their perceptions were set against a background of purposes in which intellectual development was seen as most important, though not of overriding significance. To the teachers discovery was a polymorphous concept, complex and many-sided, though not so diffuse as to be meaningless. In essence it involved children exploring situations and solving problems without following detailed instructions or standard procedures. Based on this common core, a variety of discovery approaches were seen as apposite in different contexts. There could be varying degrees of teacher initiation and of teacher guidance; the learning could be planned in advance or begin accidentally; the children could work with concrete materials or symbols or a combination of both. Discovery learning was seen to characterize a wide range of teacher-child-content transactions, though not so wide as some theorists would suggest, since, for example, project work and creative activities were not seen as discovery learning by many of the teachers. Discovery learning was seen as having significant outcomes, but more moderate ones than some educationists claimed. Teachers perceived discovery learning as an important addition to their repertoire of classroom techniques but one which had limitations too. It was important in that it promoted independence, recall, questioning, learning from experience and communication, but it was limited as a means of developing concepts or promoting knowledge acquisition. The teachers regarded discovery as valuable in many areas of the curriculum but not as some sort of panacea. All in all, a scepticism for the extreme claims made for and against discovery characterized their responses.

Though the research was far from exhaustive and is in need of replication to test and extend its conclusions, it did provide tentative evidence of a shift towards a more 'child-centred' position on the part of primary school teachers. The position held appeared to be a moderate one, and might have only existed at the level of 'ideology' and perception rather than at the level of actual classroom interaction. As Herron (1969) commented, 'we "talk" a much more impressive procedure than we actually do'. The teachers were prepared to give a measure of support to an approach to teaching and learning which promoted independence, questioning and exploration on the part of pupils. A pragmatic 'child-centred theory' was in evidence but one noticeably less extreme than that of the Froebelians.

If this 'theory' *is* held more loosely by teachers than by theorists, the challenge to the teaching profession is to develop classroom 'technologies' for realizing the acknowledged outcomes of discovery learning (Westbury, 1973). To make this development possible teachers need to demand the necessary support materials and infrastructure. They need to engage in a professional dialogue on an inter- and intra-school basis, they need to open up genuine two-way communication links with all concerned about education, and they need to be willing to sacrifice a measure of personal classroom autonomy in order to foster greater professional competence.

The study revealed, too, the utter inadequacy of current educational language in its attempts to deal with the complexities of discovery learning. Over-simple conceptualization, bold, unreal dichotomies and emotive slogans need to be replaced by a more precise language and by a more developed 'practical theory' which will address themselves to the complexities of teacher-child-content transactions which take place in classrooms.

Research workers need to play a major part in developing the language, the theory and the technologies of discovery learning, and in seeking answers to such complex practical questions as 'What is the incidence of various types of discovery learning across age-groups, schools and curriculum areas?', 'How do teachers plan and organize for learning involving discovery?', 'How do they achieve a 'mix' of teaching approaches which include teaching for discovery learning?', 'Are there any overriding constraints preventing the institutionalization of discovery learning?', 'How far is discovery effective in meeting its perceived outcomes?' To answer these and many other questions, the classroom necessarily becomes the most important arena for future research.

Until now 'there has been very little research and evaluation on Open Education aside from testimonials by exponents and reporters' (Walberg and Thomas, 1972), and this claim embraces discovery learning. Such research is urgently needed if practices of primary education are to be improved and if better, more practically useful theories are to be developed in readily communicable ways to those seeking to upgrade their pedagogy. Our 'weak commitment to empirical research as a means of dealing with our professional problems' as Walker (1973) puts it, has to be countered by the conviction that, though teaching in the final analysis may be an art, it can still be enriched by the increased understanding which accrues from empirical inquiry.

References

ANASTASIOUW, N., *et al.* (1970) 'A comparison of guided discovery, discovery and didactic teaching of kintergarten poverty children', *Amer. Educ. Res. J.*, 7, 493–510.

ASH, B., and RAPAPORT, B. (1965) *The Junior School Today.* London: National Froebel Foundation. Third Edition.

ASHTON, P., *et al.* (1972) *A Study of the Aims of Primary Education.* Mimeographed report, Teaching Research Unit, University of Birmingham School of Education.

AUSUBEL, D. (1963) *The Psychology of Meaningful Verbal Learning.* New York: Grune and Stratton.

AUSUBEL, D. (1968) *Educational Psychology: a Cognitive View.* New York: Holt, Rinehart and Winston.

BANTOCK, G. (1969) 'Discovery Methods', in Cox, C., and Dyson, A. (Eds.) *Black Paper Two.* London: Critical Quarterly Society.

BARTH, R. (1969) 'Open Education: assumptions about learning', *Educational Philosophy and Theory*, 1, 29–52.

BIGGS, E. (1965) *Mathematics in the Primary School.* London: HMSO.

BIGGS, E. (1966) 'The development of mathematical activity in primary school children', in *The Development of Mathematical Activity in Children.* London: Association of Teachers of Mathematics.

BIGGS, E. (1971) 'The role of experience in the teaching of mathematics', *The Arithmetic Teacher*, 18, 278, 285–295.

BOARDER, S., *et al.* (1964) *Aspects of Language in the Primary School.* London: National Froebel Foundation. Second Edition.

BROWN, S. (1971) 'Learning by discovery: rationale, implementation and misconceptions', *Educational Theory*, 21, 232–260.

BRUNER, J. (1961) 'The Act of Discovery', *Harvard Educ. Rev.*, 31, 21–32.

BRUNER, J. (1966) 'Some elements of discovery', in Shulman, L., and Keiscar, E. (Eds.) *Learning by Discovery.* Chicago: Rand McNally, 101–114.

Cambridge Conference (1963) *Goals for School Mathematics.* Boston: Houghton Mifflin.

FOSTER, J. (1972) *Discovery Learning in the Primary School.* London: RKP.

FROOME, S. (1970) *Why Tommy isn't Learning.* London: Tom Stacey.

FROOME, S. (1974) 'Back on the right track', *Education 3–13*, 2, 13–16.

FRIEDLANDER, B. (1965) 'A Psychologist's second thoughts on concepts, curiosity and discovery in teaching and learning', *Harvard Educ. Rev.*, 35, 18–38.

GAGNÉ, R. (1966) 'Varieties of learning and the concept of discovery', in Shulman, L., and Keislar, E. (Eds.) *Learning by Discovery*. Chicago: Rand McNally, 135–150.

GOODMAN, L., and KRUSKAL, W. (1954) 'Measures of association from cross-classification, *J. Amer. Stat. Assoc.*, 49, 732–764.

GOODMAN, L., and KRUSKAL, W. (1959) 'Measures of association for cross-classification, further discussion and references', *J. Amer. Stat. Assoc.*, 54, 123–163.

GOODMAN, L., and KRUSKAL, W. (1964) 'Approximate sampling theory', *J. Amer. Stat. Assoc.*, 58, 310–364.

HARGREAVES, D. (1972) *Interpersonal Relations and Education*. London: RKP.

HENDRIX, G. (1961) 'Learning by Discovery', *Mathematics Teaching*, 54, 290–299.

HERRON, M. (1969) 'Nature of Science: panacea or Pandora's box?', *J. Res. in Sci. Teach.*, 6, 105–107.

ISAACS, N. (1958) *Early Scientific Trends in Children*. London: National Froebel Foundation.

KERSH, B. (1964) 'Learning by discovery: what is learned?', *The Arithmetic Teacher*, 11, 224–232.

KERSH, B. (1965) 'Learning by discovery: instructional strategies, *The Arithmetic Teacher*, 12, 414–417.

KERSH, B., and WITTROCK, M. (1962) 'Learning by discovery: an interpretation of recent research', *J. Teacher Educ.*, 13, 461–468.

MARSH, L. (1970) *Alongside the Child in the Primary School*. London: Black.

MARSH, L. (1973) *Being a Teacher*. London: Black.

MORINE, G. (1969) 'Discovery modes: a criterion for teaching', *Theory into Practice*, VIII, 25–30.

MORRISETT, L. (1966) 'Further reflections', in Shulman, L., and Keislar, E. (Eds.) *Learning by Discovery*. Chicago: Rand McNally, 177–180.

PLOWDEN, B. (1967) *Children and their Primary Schools*. London: HMSO.

RICHARDS, C. (1973a) 'Third thoughts on discovery', *Educ. Rev.*, 25, 143–150.

RICHARDS, C. (1973b) 'Primary school teachers' perceptions of discovery learning'. Unpublished MEd dissertation, School of Education, University of Birmingham.

RICHARDS, C. (1974) 'Curriculum development in the English primary school—reality and possibility', *Elem. School J.*, 74, 210–219.

RICHARDS, R. (1973) 'The swinging of a pendulum: discovery science with young children', *Education 3–13*, 1, 23–28.

SCHON, D. (1971) *Beyond the Stable State*. Temple Smith: London.

SCHWAB, J. (1973) 'The practical 3: translation into curriculum', *School Rev.*, 81, 501–522.

SUCHMAN, J. (1961) 'Inquiry training: building skills for autonomous discovery', *Merrill-Palmer Quarterly*, 7, 148–169.

SUCHMAN, J. (1964) 'The Illinois studies in inquiry training', *J. Res. in Sci. Teach.*, 2, 230–232.

SZABO, S. (1967) 'Some remarks on discovery', *Mathematics Teacher*, 60, 839–842.

TAYLOR, P., et al. (1974) *Purpose, Power and Constraint in the Primary School Curriculum*. Schools Council Research Series: Macmillan Educational.

WALBERG, H., and THOMAS, S. (1972) 'Open education: a classroom validation in Great Britain and the United States', *Amer. Educ. Res. J.*, 9.

WALKER, D. (1973) 'What Curriculum Research?', *J. Curric. Studies*, 5, 58–72.

WALTERS, E. (1965) *Activity and Experience in the Junior School*. London: National Froebel Foundation, (Sixth edition).
WESTBURY, I. (1973) 'Conventional Classrooms, "Open" Classrooms and the Technology of Teaching', *J. Curric. Studies*, 5, 99–121.
WITTROCK, M. (1966) 'The learning by discovery hypothesis', in Shulman, L., and Keislar, E. (Eds.) *Learning by Discovery*. Chicago: Rand McNally, 33–76.
WORTHEN, B. (1968). 'A study of discovery and expository presentation', *J. Teacher Educ.*, 19, 223–242.

Appendix I

Learning situations take many different forms. As a result of discussions with primary school teachers the following paragraphs have been drawn up, each describing a particular learning situation. For each paragraph ask yourself: 'Is this a case of discovery learning?'

Please use the following scale and place a ring round the appropriate response at the end of each paragraph, e.g. 5 4 3 2 1.

Is this a case of discovery learning?

definitely	5
probably	4
not sure	3
probably not	2
definitely not	1

1. At the teacher's initial suggestion Jimmy (aged nine) decided to measure the speeds recorded for snails of different sizes. When he had done this using his own methods, he wrote, 'I think that size doesn't have anything to do with the speed and movement of snails'.   5 4 3 2 1

2. Frank (six) was writing a story about monsters. He wanted to use the word 'gigantic' but he couldn't spell it, so he looked at the class dictionary hung up by the teacher's desk.   5 4 3 2 1

3. At the teacher's suggestion and under her supervision Gregg (seven) compared the time taken for kettles to boil. He recorded his results as follows: 'Miss T's kettle boiled the fastest of all the kettles. Mrs M's kettle took the longest to boil. Mrs M's kettle took $4\frac{1}{2}$ minutes to boil. The school kettle took 4 minutes'.   5 4 3 2 1

4. The teacher shows Audrey (eight) how to construct a block graph illustrating the distribution of children's birthdays throughout the year. They discuss the completed graph.   5 4 3 2 1

G

5. The gift of a precision geometry set inspired Scott (nine) to experiment with drawing circles, patterns and regular polygons. In the process he taught himself some geometry.   5 4 3 2 1

6. The teacher is trying to teach Ian (ten) how to measure areas. She asks him to draw rectangles of various sizes on squared paper, to count the number of square centimetres inside each rectangle and to write that figure down as the area. Ian says he has found a quick way of finding the area of a rectangle. 'You just times how long it is by how wide it is, Miss.'   5 4 3 2 1

7. Julie (11) wanted to test the strength of various threads. After a great deal of discussion with her teacher she designed some apparatus to compare and measure strengths. She found out that a greater breaking force was required to snap string than was required to break fuse wire, cotton, or wool.   5 4 3 2 1

8. As part of a topic on 'fire' which he had chosen himself, John (10) set up a number of his own experiments to see the relative burning time of different types of matches. He recorded his results in his 'fire' booklet.   5 4 3 2 1

9. In an Oxfordshire primary school, Philip (eight) brought in a 19th century stone bottle and when he started to clean it out he found the remains of several small animals inside. The teacher helped him to identify many of these animals.   5 4 3 2 1

10. A lower junior aged seven picks up a work card on sound. This suggests that he taps several milk bottles to see what noise is produced and then suggests that he fills the bottles to varying degrees with water before tapping again. He does this and realizes that different sounds are produced when bottles are filled with varying amounts of water.   5 4 3 2 1

11. A teacher asks Bill (10) if he can see around corners or hear around corners. After a discussion the teacher tells Bill that light cannot travel around corners but sound can.   5 4 3 2 1

12. Brian (five) picks up a cardboard tube, blows down it and makes a noise. He then picks up other objects around the room and blows down them to see if they make a noise. He tells his teacher what he has done.   5 4 3 2 1

13. As part of an individual project Colin (eight) decided to find out about snakes. He got four books from the library, made notes and drew pictures. He produced an eight-page booklet on snakes.   5 4 3 2 1

14. Whilst visiting a Welsh border castle Peter (nine)
    was fascinated by the moat. He wanted to know the
    reason for it. His teacher explained that it was a
    means of defending the castle from attack.   5 4 3 2 1

15. Adrian (11) was working on a 'tea' project. As a
    result of an assignment card made out by the
    teacher he found out how much tea was carried by a
    tea clipper, he calculated how many hundred-weight
    bags this would fill and estimated how many cups of
    tea could be made from a shipload.   5 4 3 2 1

16. A group of top infants were engaged in a project on
    'Indians' sparked off by a display mounted by a
    student teacher. After talking to the group about the
    design of tepees, she gave Paula (seven) a book.
    From this Paula learnt that each Indian family had its
    own particular design.   5 4 3 2 1

17. A teacher suggests to Gary (eight) that he should look
    at the windows in the local church and should note
    especially their similarities and their differences.
    He returns with drawings of the windows and
    remarks on the different shapes. The teacher asks
    why this is so. After thinking a while he suggests
    that perhaps the windows were built at different
    times by different people.   5 4 3 2 1

18. By showing her some marionettes he had made
    himself, a teacher described to Pat how fashions had
    changed during Tudor and Stuart times. Pat (nine)
    drew pictures to illustrate these changes.   5 4 3 2 1

19. Simon (11) was accustomed to improvising using
    Orff-type instruments. He wanted to invent a piece
    of 'Chinese' music to fit into a project and after
    experimenting he found a scale which he described
    as 'spooky'.   5 4 3 2 1

20. As a result of a visit Eileen (10) picked up a sprig
    of holly and decided to base some work around it.
    When she returned to school, she embroidered the
    sprig as part of her follow-up. The design was her
    own, although she did ask the teacher for some help
    with an embroidery technique.   5 4 3 2 1

21. After a television programme on horses a peripatetic
    music teacher spent some time with Julie (seven)
    suggesting lines of approach and helping her to
    compose tunes for the various movements of the
    horses.   5 4 3 2 1

22. Tony (five) became interested in shells after the
    teacher had mounted a display. He took some shells
    to the sand tray and made patterns by using the
    shells.   5 4 3 2 1

23. After a TV programme on cave paintings a teacher
    got David (eight) to paint a picture on a piece of slate. 5 4 3 2 1

24. In a craftwork lesson Peter (11) made a paper
    sculpture by following the teacher's verbal
    instructions one step at a time.   5 4 3 2 1

25. In teaching Barbara the recorder the teacher plays
    the first phrase of 'London's burning' while Barbara
    (nine) fingers the notes without actually playing.
    Then she in turn plays the phrase the teacher has
    played. In this way she comes to learn the whole of
    'London's burning'.   5 4 3 2 1

26. Nigel (six) wanted to make a boat. With a little help
    from his teacher he made a boat out of cardboard
    boxes and cotton reels.   5 4 3 2 1

27. As a result of a school-sponsored balloon race a
    junior class became interested in balloons. The
    teacher was particularly interested in modelling and
    as a result of his guidance John (10) made three
    models of flying balloons based on pictures in
    reference books.   5 4 3 2 1

28. The teacher asked her class how many different ways
    they could move. Joan (five) found three different
    ways; Peter found four ways.   5 4 3 2 1

29. Lynn made a collection of leaves and twigs and set up
    a display in the classroom. Her teacher helped her
    draw up a list of words connected with her display,
    which she then used in writing a poem.   5 4 3 2 1

30. Christine (seven) liked poetry. She read some poems
    and on 6 November composed a poem on Bonfire
    Night without any help or prompting from the
    teacher.   5 4 3 2 1

31. Angela (10) was interested in poetry and went to the
    teacher one day with a book on Shakespeare's plays.
    She said 'Most of the plays in here are nothing, only
    poetry. I don't understand them but I can see they're
    poetry—they read like poetry anyway even though
    most of them have no rhymes.'   5 4 3 2 1

32. Rosalind and Susan are talking to a student teacher.
    Rosalind says 'Her name's "Murphy" and my
    name's "Murray". It starts and ends the same—
    it's got the same number of letters. Oh! Only two
    letters are different.'   5 4 3 2 1

33. Alan (11) described to the class the experiment he
    had just completed. At the teacher's suggestion but
    using his own particular methods he had compared
    the ways in which different materials dried. His
    recorded results included drying curves for each
    material and calculations of the water content.   5 4 3 2 1

Appendix 2

Below is a list of statements which have been applied to discovery learning with children of average and above average ability. Please read them carefully and then indicate using the following scale the extent to which you agree with them by placing a ring round the appropriate number, e.g. 5 4 3 2 1

Entirely agree 5
Agree 4
Neither agree nor disagree 3
Disagree 2
Entirely disagree 1

1. Discovery learning leads to children acquiring a
body of useful knowledge.   5   4   3   2   1

2. Discovery learning leads to children acquiring
firmly-based concepts.   5   4   3   2   1

3. Discovery learning results in children remembering
experiences and their significance more readily.   5   4   3   2   1

4. Discovery learning leads to children being interested
in learning for its own sake.   5   4   3   2   1

5. Discovery learning results in children developing
independence in thought and action.   5   4   3   2   1

6. Discovery learning leads to children being confident
in their ability to solve problems.   5   4   3   2   1

7. Discovery learning results in children developing a
questioning attitude.   5   4   3   2   1

8. Discovery learning produces future citizens who
will be capable of adjusting to their changing
environment.   5   4   3   2   1

9. Discovery learning results in children developing
new ideas and new ways of looking at things.   5   4   3   2   1

10. Discovery learning results in children being able to
apply skills and principles in new contexts.   5   4   3   2   1

11. Discovery learning leads children to develop more
positive attitudes towards school.   5   4   3   2   1

12. Discovery learning results in informal, relaxed
pupil-teacher relationships.   5   4   3   2   1

13. Discovery learning leads to children co-operating
with others in solving common problems.   5   4   3   2   1

14. Discovery learning leads to children communicating
their experiences in a variety of ways.   5   4   3   2   1

15. Discovery learning leads to children taking some
    responsibility for their own learning.   5 4 3 2 1

16. Discovery learning results in purposeful learning
    adapted to the child's needs and interests.   5 4 3 2 1

17. Discovery learning leads children to learn from their
    own experiences in both school and out-of-school
    contexts.   5 4 3 2 1

An Exercise in Managing Curriculum Development in a Primary School

Peter Evans and
Maurice Groarke (Devon County Authority)

Introduction

Curriculum has been neatly defined by Johnson (1969) as a 'structured series of intended learning outcomes.' At whatever level the curriculum is discussed, whatever theories are promulgated and whatever organizational ploys are devised the essential substance of curriculum is 'children doing things.' We are practitioners, we are teachers, we teach in school. We accept that we are responsible for what children do and how they do it. The maintenance of curriculum momentum is our concern and so the intentional thrust comes from us, that is the outcome, the effect, of what the children do, on the children, will be essentially our intentions for them. Yet we are not completely autonomous. Our intentions are not merely what we as individuals feel should be done but represent our interpretation of societal demands made on schools in general. The debate about the aims of education goes on but for the day-to-day activities of a school certain basic assumptions have to be made about those aims. For a school to function at all an elementary framework of priorities, recognizable as fundamental and authentic aims, must form the backcloth to action. We must assume, for example, that all children should be taught to read, that all children should be numerate, that all children should be able to express, in written or verbal form, whatever the situational context demands of them. We could call this framework the ultimate outcome pattern, and whatever the children do in school, the detailed moments of the curriculum are to be set against this general web of expectancies.

An interesting question now arises: How does the staff of a school convert this web of expectancies into action? How is the content methodology and form of the curriculum decided upon? Assuming that this is not some kind of self-perpetuating organic process, and that it is not mere chance or a set of fortuitous minor modifications that produces the ultimate curriculum substance, then it should be possible to study what does actually happen with a view to identifying what is good and effective practice and what is not. A body of knowledge might then become available for teachers to refer to so that each and every school, in terms of the process of curriculum innovation, would not have to start from scratch and would not end up 'working in the dark'. Owen (1969) has pointed out,

> 'How the school takes over an innovation, has not yet, in Britain, been studied at any great depth.'

This paper is one contribution.[1] It describes and analyses what happened when the staff of one particular school attempted to re-think and re-formulate one aspect of the school curriculum, over a period of three years.

The school was a nine-class junior and infants' school. Evans and Groarke, respectively headteacher and teacher-in-charge of the Area Special Class, were jointly responsible for initiating, leading and recording the exercise. Participants were the eight remaining members of staff and three teachers from other schools. All were full-time teachers and in various ways and in varying degrees, all contributed to the progress of the exercise. The curriculum aspect was that of language development and, as it subsequently evolved, language development in relation to cognitive development.

An Innovatory Climate?

Change is best observed in its effects. The causes of change are often elusive and explanations depend on hindsight interpretations. Scientists try to record it, psychologists try to measure it, sociologists hypothesize about it and educationalists are not sure where its impetus originates.

> 'We know almost nothing about the sources of new ideas in education, whether these are largely conceived in the schools to be taken up or promoted by outside bodies, or whether most of the new ideas in education are generated outside the schools' (Hoyle, 1971).

[1] For a full account see Evans, P., and Groarke, M. (1974). 'Language for Learning: an intra-school exercise in curriculum development with in-service education'. (Unpublished.) Available from the authors for consultation.

It is difficult to pinpoint the origin of an idea. It is even more difficult to pinpoint what it is exactly that transforms the idea into a form of action. We find it difficult to trace the point of origin of the firm commitment to initiate a planned exercise in curriculum innovation that we made, but we can say that those origins were connected with an attitude of mind.

We were concerned. We were dissatisfied with what we were doing for the children in our charge. We were concerned that the NFER report, *The Trend of Reading Standards* (Start and Wells, 1972) showed that the number of illiterate and semi-literate pupils leaving our schools had not only not remained constant but might actually have increased since 1960. We were bothered that the National Child Development Study, *From Birth to Seven* (1972) showed that the educational system was making no headway against the deprived social backgrounds of the children and that the chances of an unskilled manual worker's child being a poor reader at seven were six times greater than those of a professional worker's child. We were concerned that all indications pointed to the fact that the biggest single influence on a child's progress through the educational system remained his father's occupation. We had no reason to believe that our school was any different, was more to blame, than other primary schools in the country since consideration of county and national norms gave us no disparaging comparisons. But we were concerned that, looking nationally, so much appeared to be happening and yet so little was going on.

Our dissatisfactions fermented at two levels. The first, the latent level, was probably no more than the interest and concern many teachers show in the nature of their work and the needs of the children whom they teach. The second level, which we consider far more important, was the level of manifest concern. This involves a deliberate intention to be concerned. Manifest concern is the antithesis of complacency. It is also quite different in kind to latent concern because it focuses general feelings of inadequacy and half-formed, intuitive, awareness of needs, on to the more definitive ground of authenticated research. To the soft aura of informal suspicion that something is wrong, it brings the hard edge of factual evidence. The original impulse may be spontaneous but the development of the manifestly concerned attitude of mind has to be deliberately nurtured and encouraged. An essential corollary to manifest concern is manifest action and this could be the reason why latent concerns remain thick on the ground. Sessions to deal with latent concerns have to be prompted. At least one person has to be a dedicated student of educational literature and it helps to have a second person in the group similarly aware of what is going on.

Beginnings

Over a period of three years there was no particular sense of direction in our latent concern sessions. We ranged far and wide over a bewildering variety of topics and members of staff contributed much or little according to their own personal attitudes, beliefs and special interests. We were struggling with ideas, with methods, with philosophies and aspirations and sometimes we waded in shallow water and sometimes deep. The Head was not then consciously attempting to generate an atmosphere that would prepare and predispose the staff towards innovation, but creative leadership in curriculum matters was an important element within his concept of the headship role. This approach was not without its difficulties. There was a limit to the number of after school meetings that could be called. Teachers, mentally weary after their day in the classroom were not easily motivated to remain on the premises so it became (almost) a recognized procedure for the head to turn each informal meeting of the staff, at breaks and after meal times, into formal sessions. The degree of participation varied from teacher to teacher and at times there were complaints and strong reactions against 'always talking shop'. It was also difficult on occasions to avoid arousing the feeling that emphasis on the need for change was not more than adverse criticism of current practices. Also, because directed discussion is necessarily selective in terms of subject matter, there were times when individual teachers felt that some of their worries were being ignored or shouldered out. However, the general willingness to share in the debates was forthcoming and perhaps the removal of such irksome chores as keeping record books, collecting National Savings money, collecting school photograph money or biscuit money, also helped foster a readiness to co-operate.

The pay-off came gradually. Individual teachers set out to change their classroom practices and were able to offer examples and stimulation to others. One teacher, for example, introduced the 'Stott Reading Kit' (Stott, 1958) into his own reading programmes. He was then able, through the framework of the formal sessions already established, to present an introduction to Stott to the rest of the staff and eventually the Kit was incorporated into the basic reading curriculum of the entire school. Small change can be a good preparation for large scale change.

'. . . participation in small change, rather than observation of it, is the only model upon which the practitioner can base his response to larger demands.' (Owen, 1969, *op. cit.*)

We feel now that the products of our formal sessions at this stage were a necessary preliminary to the greater demands the full scale innovatory exercise was going to make on our resources as teachers and individuals. Although the strategy of fostering an incisive level of educational debate was never 100 per cent successful, it meant at least that the atmosphere was educationally fertile in that deep research findings could be presented and seriously considered.

Why Language Development?
Our formal sessions covered many aspects of the curriculum. The emergence of language as our major concern was something of a 'fluke'. Searching the local library for something to read Evans came across *Social Class Language and Education* (Lawton, 1968). This book made a deep impression on Evans and also made a similar impression on other members of staff who later read it. It made this impression because the book seemed to focus on the basic stumbling block that we had always come up against in our formal sessions. Whatever aspect of the curriculum we discussed we had tended always to arrive at the same core problem, that is, the stubborn inevitability of the national reading norms. However enthusiastically we approached new ideas, however we modified and tailored the curriculum, our judgement of the evidence led us to believe that the educational opportunities and subsequent life-chances of a large majority of the children were limited by some failure within the educational system. There was something the schools were doing or not doing. For many children the best was just not good enough or was not of the right kind. We understood the general thesis about social class effects in school. We had accepted the usual explanations for this—the lack of books in the home, the lack of parental interest in school aims, lack of genuine parental contact with the schools, inadequate housing and environmental conditions working against stable intellectual and emotional growth—all the implications of the 'culture clash' hypothesis. What we could never decide was just what the schools should be able to do about it. There was always the feeling, the disheartening feeling, that all the curriculum innovations we engineered only altered expectancies around the edges, leaving the central problem untouched. Lawton, by introducing us to the work of Bernstein, appeared to show us that the central problem was a language problem and this jerked our thinking into a new range of insights

because it dropped the issue right on to our particular plate. Immediately it became a *teacher* problem and curriculum innovation to meet the problem became a possibility. After all, language development is a central teacher concern. Success within the English education system depends largely on the ability to manipulate language in written and spoken forms. It is slightly premature to quote Bernstein at this stage in our description of the exercise, but we will do so because he makes the point so succinctly.

'For the school is necessarily concerned with the transmission and development of universalistic orders of meaning. The school is concerned with making explicit—and elaborating through language —principles and operations as these apply to objects (the science subjects) and persons (the arts subjects). . . The school is attempting to transmit un-commonsense knowledge, i.e. public knowledge realised through various "meta-languages". This knowledge is what I have called universalistic . . . The introduction of the child to the universalistic meanings of public forms of thought is not "compensatory education"; *it is education.*' (Bernstein, 1970.)

It is not possible here to describe fully the long process by which we forged our understanding of research into language until we reached the point of planned action. This whole development is described and analysed in the full account we have already written.[1] But several points can be made.

The ideas generated by Lawton began to dominate our formal sessions. Evans prepared further notes on the book, résumés of parts of it, for general staff circulation. He also prepared slides and taped material to illustrate some of the more obvious points. This material was presented to the staff as a whole and subsequently presented to a series of meetings with the parents. This not only attempted to inform parents of the significance of child-parent language interaction but also deepened staff knowledge of it. Teachers began to examine their own practices in the field of language curriculum in terms of the new insights gained from Lawton and from attempts to read some of the original Bernstein work. Our reading was very important to us because, although we felt very strongly that we were 'on to something important', we were far from clear as to where our inquiries would lead us and what would evolve in practicable curriculum terms. We read what books and articles we could find about language fairly indiscriminately and this led us to writers like Vigotsky and Chomsky who, apart from a few

[1] See footnote, page 104.

glittering insights, we found almost incomprehensible. Out of all our reading there eventually emerged three books that focused our thinking and gave us guidelines for action.

Around that time we came across the series, *Primary Socialization Language and Education*, published by Routledge and Kegan Paul and edited by Bernstein (1970). Despite Bernstein's own misgivings about the book in the Foreword to it, it was Volume III in the series by the Gahagans (1970) that was important for us. The book reassured us that we were interpreting the Bernstein work in the way that teachers would have to interpret it, and demonstrated the kinds of curriculum activities that such interpretations might lead to. About the same time we also made a detailed study of *Speech and the Development of Mental Processes in the Child* by Luria and Yudovich (1971). This clarified for us the link between language development and cognitive growth, which seemed to us the 'secret unknown factor' that had so far eluded us. Although we realized no research evidence is ever conclusive, we decided, after much study and discussion, that if we were to attempt to construct a new language curriculum the link with cognitive growth would be accepted as a working hypothesis. We felt that somewhere we had to make a decisive stand, otherwise our formal sessions could go on for ever and nothing concrete result. It was around this time that we made a declaration of intent to proceed with the exercise. We, as instigators, agreed to do this first. The proposition was then put to the staff as a whole and it was accepted. The exercise was on.

However, mention must be made here of *Teaching Disadvantaged Children in the Pre-School* by Bereiter and Engelmann (1966). This book surprised us and significantly altered our methodology. It surprised us because we had already heard of its authors through the media and reading chance articles. We had an impression of them as rather brutal and callous in their treatment of children and we did not expect to find much in their work appropriate to our needs. Yet we did find that their introduction to that book coincided with our own thinking to a remarkable extent. Their analysis of language forms and structure also gave us an excellent basic framework against which to build our own sequential programmes.

The Exercise Itself
The decision to conduct the exercise cut the edges of our concerns into limited shape. We accepted limitations because we badly needed an end product. Language development is a vast area and there were obviously many good books and articles, research findings and theoretical papers

we had not read. But it is also a very important area (important, that is, for the children) and we realized that if child-affecting practices were to be our objective, somewhere along the line we had to call a halt to deliberations and make some decisions. So we defined the objectives of the exercise. These were:

1. To introduce into the curriculum, programmes of language development designed to promote codes of speech considered to be essential to the development of the mental processes.

2. To test the proposition that participation in such an exercise offers the best medium for in-service education of teachers.

3. To make a constructive response to the assertion 'How the school takes over an innovation, has not yet, in Britain, been studied at any great depth' (Owen, 1969, *op. cit.*).

We also worked in accordance with certain definitions. Curriculum we considered to mean 'what is intended to be learned'; the 'structured series of intended learning outcomes' of Johnson (1969, *op. cit.*). We considered 'curriculum development' had in fact taken place when four conditions had been met. These were:

1. When there existed an unambiguous statement of *what* were to be the intended learning outcomes.

2. When there existed a statement of justification *why* the children were to learn what was intended.

3. When the elements involved in *how* the children were to learn what was intended—methods, materials, organizational strategies— were prepared in detail and were seen to be manageable by teachers.

4. When the innovation was institutionalized; that is, when the teachers were aware of the *what*, *why*, and *how* elements and it was demonstrated to their satisfaction that the new approach was superior to that which existed before, to an extent that promotes their genuine and continuing support.

Our second objective, the testing of the exercise as a medium of in-service education for the participants, was clearly specified as such because of our growing dissatisfaction with what was then currently on offer to us by way of in-service opportunities. These seemed to us quite inadequate, often irrelevant to our own and to the children's needs and seemed to be based on a fallacious conception of the nature and purpose of in-service education. We defined in-service education as the process which would enable teachers to 'become open to a wider variety of information; capable of pursuing a wider range of goals; versatile in producing new ideas, knowledge and techniques of value both to the group and to others; increasingly effective in exchanging things of value with others' (Mills, 1967). We differentiated between 'in-service training' and 'in-service education' but we did not completely deny the usefulness of the former. It was considered that meeting the *what, why* and *how* conditions for curriculum development would require and generate a strong element of in-service education, whereas the *what* and *how* conditions could well involve in-service training elements.

A more detailed analysis of the two terms is contained in the full report of the exercise.[1] Suffice it to say here, we were taking education at its face value; we were accepting that the criteria by which we recognize that children are being educated—the exhibition of a degree of transformation in behaviour or performance—would be the criteria by which we could judge teacher education. As 'physician heal thyself' so, 'educator educate thyself'.

A statement of our objectives was written down and displayed on the staff-room information board as Stage I of our procedural model. Staff were invited to participate as they wished.

The Model

Having decided on participation in a formal exercise and having specified certain objectives, there was now a need for a plan of action. Evans, therefore, produced the Procedural Model. He was concerned especially with maintaining momentum and ensuring that some form of sequential intent would underlie our actions. The existence of a procedural model was a self-imposed discipline and could be criticized on the grounds that it set limitations on the potential for open-ended products, but there was good evidence, within our experience, that diffuseness could result in inaction, as we had seen well-intentioned working parties 'fizzle away' through lack of planning.

Our Model split the exercise into 12 stages. These were:

Stage 1: Setting the climate.

Stage 2: Justification for 'language development' as the theme of the exercise.

Stage 3: Examination of current practices.

Stage 4: Formal study of the literature.

Stage 5: Testing to obtain evidence of children's speech in a situation demanding 'mediate' responses, that is, responses required within a

[1] See footnote on page 104.

specific context determined by someone other than the child himself, and which demand the exercise of the intellect. In the playground the child may make comments—'immediate responses'—with reference to situations of his own choosing. In the classroom, if he is to profit from the learning situation, he has to make 'mediate responses' in situations directed by the teacher.

Stage 6: Planning, producing and using a pilot programme.

Stage 7: Second Test to provide evidence to assess the effect of the pilot programme over one term.

Stage 8: Decision to abandon/modify/extend the exercise.

Stage 9: Planning, producing additional programmes.

Stage 10: Third Test to provide evidence to assess the effect of the four programmes which were eventually produced.

Stage 11: Decision to abandon/modify/institutionalize the system.

Stage 12: Dissemination.

Progress of the Exercise

Stage 1. Setting the climate
All our formal sessions on language development were taken as part of this stage. This included our unsystematic reading and our preparation for and presentation of the Parent Teacher Association meetings on language. We also produced a number of display charts on our objectives and definitions.

A document entitled 'Why Bother' was produced. This brought together material from our reading and set out the factors that led to the exercise. Essentially this described our discontent with the number of children who benefited little from six years in school and the document also analysed our discontent with local provision for in-service education.

Arising from the concern with in-service education we produced another document entitled 'Why an Exercise?' This suggested there could well be a siamese-twin relationship between curriculum development and in-service education. It was argued that this hypothesis might best be tested, if we participated in an exercise intended to translate theory and research findings into classroom practices.

Stage 2. Justification for 'language development' as the theme of the exercise
We collected together recordings of the speech of adults and children over an age range of four to 80. Some recordings were already in existence in the school archives. These were recordings made by children of adults and other children, as part of their project work. What surprised us about these recordings was the extent to which we

had failed to extract from them quite important educational implications as to language development. We now found that our studies and readings had affected our way of listening to the spoken word and we found that sections of these older tapes represented significant illustrations of what the researchers were saying.

Our justification for concentrating the exercise on language development was argued in a document we produced entitled, 'Why Language?' This document condensed from the literature a list of causes considered to result in lowered educational performance. We attempted to isolate those causes about which the school might be able to do something and presented a conclusion that language development appeared the one area where the school might find its best opportunity for affecting the cycle of poor educational attainment which teachers found in their children.

Stage 3. Examination of current practices

By the time we reached this stage teachers were already examining critically, their own practices in the area of language. There was a general concern about language, a mixture of new practices and some quite fruitful feedback for our formal sessions.

More specific evidence was provided by recording teachers at work and a recording was also made by the Head intervening specifically in an infant class situation attempting to prompt language responses. Both these tapes were referred to during the exercise later on and our study of them was not confined to this stage. As in the case of the tapes mentioned in Stage 2 above, later reference to them proved most interesting. Again we found that the more the exercise progressed the more acute we had become in listening to speech. When, later on in the exercise, Evans again listened to the tape he had made with the infants, he was able to find quite significant errors in his own teaching technique. In fact this later analysis convinced us, much to Evans' chagrin and to our mutual surprise that certain of the prompt procedures he used would restrict rather than enhance the children's use of language. Evans was so intrigued by this discovery that he later produced a document analysing the whole of this tape in the new light. This document was displayed along with the rest for staff to read, and was entitled 'Examination of Current Practices'.

Stage 4. Formal study of the literature

Our study of the relevant literature formed a continuing background to the exercise. We always considered this to be most important. Several

H

copies of our four basic books, mentioned earlier, were purchased and staff were encouraged to read them. A great deal of our formal discussion time was devoted to them and the initiators made notes and résumés of whole sections of them. These were available for staff to read also. We kept a close watch on the book reviews in various journals and used the NUT library and the Exeter University education library as resource centres when we wanted copies.

Stage 5. Testing to obtain evidence of children's speech in a situation demanding a 'mediate' response
We took it as axiomatic that, before any curriculum innovation could be institutionalized, there had to be some form of evaluation. We had to have some kind of objective measure of children's speech in a situation calling for a 'mediate' response both before we changed the curriculum and after, because there was always a possibility that, even after all our work, the changed curriculum might be no more effective or even less effective than current practices. We were very wary of being caught in the trap of change for change's sake.

The decision to test faced us with a whole range of problems. We had neither the skill nor the training to devise a standardized test. Nor was it practicable, certainly in terms of time, to use tests already on the market. Our familiarity with published language tests was most sketchy and none seemed to satisfy our criteria, which was for some kind of measurement of intellectual functioning linked to language development which could be carried out simply and quickly.

We were also aware of other difficulties. We could not provide a control group for purposes of comparison. If the programmes were to be effective we could not deny any children in the school the opportunity of using them merely for the sake of our exercise. Nor could we hope to measure or counter any 'Hawthorne effect'. Indeed, as teachers, if our concentration on language development was itself producing such an effect, then we would welcome it even though, in pure experimental terms, it could be clouding the results.

Eventually we produced 'The Car Test'. This was a verbal test, given individually, estimated to take about 10 minutes per child but untimed. It involved the use of two toy cars, a model roadway and one figure. It set out to establish categories of 'able' and 'non-able' performance in 11 areas. These were:

Total verbal output
Number of sentence units or utterances

Mean length of utterance
Discrimination
Classification
Description
Verbalizing on on-going situation
Verbalizing an anticipated situation
Planning speech
Voluntary speech.

All these designations were culled from the pages of the books we had studied. The Test was given to 30 infant children, for the purpose of the exercise, and also to other children throughout the school, including the Special Class. Every test was recorded, so that when the testing was finished we had abundant taped material which we could use eventually to assess our programmes and which we could also study to further our investigations of children using language in the 'mediate' situation.

Stage 6. Planning, producing and using a pilot programme
The next task was to agree on the content and format of a pilot programme, and to plan the organizational structure for its implementation. The Area Special Class was concentrating on programmes in line with the work of the Gahagans with additional lesson practices gleaned from the Luria and Yudovich book. Groarke typed out a series of lesson formats for this work and these formed the basis of a collection to which other teachers added sheets. After much discussion and experimentation there finally emerged our, initial, Prompt Programme.

This programme consisted of around 40 separate items and each teacher was asked to contribute materials and lesson format for four items. The best of these were selected to form the nucleus of the programme.

The approach was individual and each child was placed in a situation demanding verbal response to prompts in association with one or more everyday toys or objects. Even organizing for groups of 10 children at a time it was not possible, of course, to locate every child with one teacher so it was agreed that a system of cross-age tutoring would be used. Older children, from the top class, were each given instructions in the use of the programme and were made responsible for working with one infant. One or sometimes two teachers would be available to co-ordinate the work and take part in the tutoring. It was hoped that the cross-age tutoring would benefit both groups.

Here is an example 'Prompt Sheet' taken from the 'Prompt Programme'.

Apparatus: Piano

Prompts	Type of response to be encouraged
Introduction You try to play the piano and tell me all about it	Let the child play and say anything he wishes.
Naming What is this? What is this?	This is a piano. This is a key (show a door-key) This is a piano key
What are these? What is this (other parts of the piano)?	These are piano keys This is a........etc.
Describing Tell me something about this key Tell me something about this key Tell me something else about this key	This key is white This key is black This key is short
Tell me two things about this key Tell me two things about this key Tell me what this key is *not* (white) Tell me what this key is *not* (black) Tap a key that is ... white/black/ not white/not black/not short/ not long	This key is black and short This key is long and white This key is not black This key is not white
Verbalising (on-going situation) Tap a white key. Tell me what you are doing Tap a black key. Tell me what you are doing Tap all the keys, one at a time	I am tapping a white key I am tapping a black key I am tapping the keys one at a time
Tap a lot of keys all together Make it play loud. Tell me what you are doing	I am tapping a lot of keys I am making it play loud(ly)

Prompts	Type of response to be encouraged

Make it play another way. Tell me
what you are doing   I am making it play quiet(ly)
Make it tinkle like a bell   I am making it play like a bell
Make it sound like thunder   I am making it sound like
                                 thunder

Go on, play it, and tell me what
you are doing

Verbalizing in a situation that has to be imagined
What sort of a noise will it make
if I do this (tap heavily above   It will make a loud thundery
left hand key)?   noise
What sort of a noise will it make
if I do this (tap lightly above   It will make a quiet tinkling
several right hand keys)?   noise
You try it and find out. Were you
right? Get your fingers ready, then
tell me what will happen. Do it,   It will make a loud noise, etc.
were you right?

Narrative planning
When you are all ready to sing,   She sits down. She opens the
me what Mrs Cornish does at the   lid . . . etc.
piano

Voluntary speech
Tell me all you can about this piano
Have you got one at home etc.?

Questioning
I've asked you a lot of questions
Now you ask me some about this
piano
How does it make a noise?
(Show inside the piano and explain.
Ask child to explain)
What are those things (pedals) for?
How can you find out? That's
right, try them

Prompts	*Type of response to be encouraged*

Talk-through
Go on, have a good play with it
Tell me what you are doing   Child 'talks-through' what he
                                    is doing

(The 'prompts' are not, of course,
intended to be a script from which
no deviations are permitted.
Whatever the child says, so long
as it is relevant, should be
pursued.)

Stage 7. Second test to provide evidence to assess the effect of the pilot programme over one term
The Car Test was given again. Again all tests were recorded. A document was prepared setting out all the results in discursive and in tabulated form, with detailed records of comparisons between individual performances on the first test and the second test. This evidence was used as a basis for discussions held during Stage 8.

Stage 8. Decision to abandon/modify/extend the exercise
In actual fact, around this time, we had to deviate from the Model. The Test was given in late July and if full evaluation of the Test results had been left until September we would not have been able to embark on Stage 9 until that time and a whole term could have been wasted while the programmes were produced. Also by this time we had read the Bereiter and Engelmann book and were excited by the insights we gained into actual language structure. It was becoming much clearer what kinds of programmes we would have to produce. We made the bold decision to extend the programmes before the Test results were formulated so our evaluation of the Tests, our discussion of the results and our preparation for future programmes were going on all together. It was not an ideal situation but we accepted it as inevitable with the time available to us. The Test results subsequently confirmed our decision as the right one.

Stage 9. Planning, producing additional programmes
We kept the Prompt Programme, modifying and extending it.
   We produced three completely new types of programme, together

with a detailed Teacher's Manual to go with each. These programmes were called:

The Chart Programme—23 large charts
The Slide Programme—81 slides
The Kit Programme—boxes containing 37 small items.

For each programme item the Teacher's Manual explains:

the *what*—the intended learning outcome for each session
the *why*—the reason for each intended learning outcome
the *how*—the techniques and organization of the lesson.

Organizational strategies were devised by which all the four programmes could be put into effect.

This is one section of the 'Chart Programme Teacher's Manual' Chart 19.

The illustrations on the very large chart are as follows—from left to right, numbered 1, 2, 3, 4, a big white house, a big yellow house, a small white house, a small yellow house.

WHAT (is to be taught): the word 'or'

WHY (is this to be taught). The deductive process very often leads not to a final conclusion but to another set of possibilities or questions. Using 'or' expresses the existence of an open-ended alternative making clear the departure from the idea that there must always be one final solution. Children in school are dominated by the desire to be right so that the presentation of the idea of possibilities is very important.

HOW (is this to be taught)

Teacher: What is this?
Children or Child: This is a house.
T: What are these?
C: These are houses.
T: I am thinking of a house that is big.
Which house am I thinking about?
C: You are thinking about house number 1.
T: No, I am thinking about house number 2. Try again.
C: You are thinking about house number 2.
T: No, I was thinking about house number 1. Try again.
I am thinking about a house that is big. Which house am I thinking about?

Explain: there are two big houses; if a child fails to make the correct response the teachers says:
I am thinking about house number 1 *or* house number 2.

T: Let's try another question like that. I am thinking about a house that is small.

C: You are thinking about house number 3 *or* house number 4.

T: I am thinking about a house that is white. Which one am I thinking about?

C: You are thinking about house number 1 *or* house number 3.

T: I am thinking about a house that is yellow. Which one?

C: You are thinking about house number 2 or house number 4.

T: I am thinking about a house that is *not* big. Which one?

C: You are thinking about house number 3 or house number 4.

T: I am thinking about a house that is *not* white. Which one?
I am thinking about house number 2 or house number 4 (and so on).

T: I am thinking about a house that is big and white.

C: You are thinking about house number 1 *or.* . . .

T: Listen and think. . . .
I am thinking about a house that is big and white.

C: You are thinking about house number 1 (and so on).

Revision exercises for Chart 19
(To give practice in the use of the word in association with active and tactile stimuli).

1. All children find an object with one common attribute, e.g. find something round/flat/white/hollow/made of wood, etc.

2. Each child makes naming statement and attribute statement.
    e.g. This is a box. This box is made of wood.

3. *Teacher:* I am thinking of something round. What am I thinking of?
    Child or Children: I don't know.

4. *Teacher:* Put on the desk all the round things I might be thinking about. Tell me of a round thing I might be thinking of.
    Children: You are thinking of a tin-lid *or* a coin *or* a counter, etc.
    Repeat with other sets of objects.

5. *T:* All sit down. What are you doing?
    C: We are all sitting down.
    T: All stand up. What are you doing?
    C: We are all standing up.

T: I want you to stand up *or* sit down.
Each child names his own action.
Repeat for lying, kneeling, walking, etc.

The slide programme
The Slide Programme is identical to the Chart Programme except that several slides, rather than one chart, are used for teaching each of the words and phrases making a total of 88 slides. The advantages of the slides over the charts were thought to be: ease of storage; speedy setting up of the materials which were permanently kept in proper order in two magazines; quick means of copying the materials; the novelty of the AVA room for the children; their interest in operating the projector themselves.

The kit programme
Here is an example of one exercise from the Kit Programme.

Exercise 63

WHAT: the words *on, over, under.*

WHY: description of the position of one object in relation to that of another is commonly used and refines concepts by the use of more explicit language.

HOW:

T: Put a red cube *on* the table. Say, The red cube is *on* the table.
T: Put a red cube *on* the table. Say, The red cube is *on* the table.
C: The red cube is *on* the table.
T: Put the cube on the floor. Where is the cube?
C: The cube is *on* the floor.
T: Put the lid *over* the cube. Say, The lid is *over* the cube.
C: The lid is *over* the cube.
T: Take out a yellow cube. Put it *under* the red cube.
Where is the yellow cube?
C: The yellow cube is *under* the red cube.
T: Where is the red cube?
C: The red cube is *over* the yellow cube.
(repeat with different coloured cubes and counters).

TEST: Language *reception*

T: Put a black cube on the table.

Put a white cube over the black cube.
Put a yellow cube under the white cube.
(Teacher does this and compares models)

TEST: Language *production*

T: to individual child—You tell us what to do. You do it as well.
(Compare child's model with his instructions.)

Stage 10. Third test to provide evidence to assess the effect of the (four) programmes
The Car Test was given again. All tests were again recorded.

One tape was edited so that each child's initial performance on the Test could be heard immediately followed by his later performance. Another tape was prepared, including items of special significance and humorous insights, for dissemination purposes outside the school.

A document was prepared listing all results from the three tests and these results were subjected to many kinds of analysis and evaluation. This evaluation was done as accurately and thoroughly as we could but we realized only too keenly our weakness as statisticians.

Stage 11. Decision to abandon/modify/institutionalize the system
A formal meeting was held at which there was a unanimous and immediate decision to continue the use of the programmes. Further discussion led to more detailed suggestions, and agreement. It was decided:

1. All four programmes would continue in use with the original test group until July 1973.

2. The infants would continue to use the Slide, Chart and Prompt Programmes until July 1973.

3. The Juniors would continue to use the Slide and Chart Programmes until July 1973.

4. From September 1973 the infants would use the Slide and Prompt Programmes during time-tabled sessions.

5. From September 1973 programmes would be used with Juniors at the discretion of their teachers. Here it was assumed that most of the children would in fact complete the programmes while still in the infant department.

6. The system would be continued until somebody produced superior methods and materials or until some new factor, within our own experience, led us to change our decision.

7. The Area Special Class would continue to use the Slide and Kit programmes together with selected aspects of the Gahagans' programmes.

Stage 12. Dissemination
Evans and Groarke agreed they would write a complete account of the exercise, to include a description of how it developed, a statement on the understanding of the research as it emerged, copies of the programmes and an analytical commentary on the problems such an exercise presents. The expectation was that this document might be of use to other schools and other staffs contemplating a similar approach to in-service education and curriculum innovation.

Evaluating the Exercise
This evaluation is the product of the participants' reactions on the exercise. It is necessarily subjective. To focus our evaluation we returned to our three objectives and tested intention against fulfilment.

Objective 1: To introduce into the curriculum, programmes of language development designed to promote codes of speech considered to be essential to the development of the mental processes.

As to the all-important link between language and mental development we had done our best. We had studied the most pertinent literature we could find and interpreted it in the light of our own education, the knowledge we had of children and our consensual view of societal demands. We had found some of the literature difficult to read and to understand and since we were 10 different individuals it could be expected that our understanding varied one from another. We could have no way of measuring this. However, we had forged some level of general understanding and we had been decisive enough to turn theory into action and produce our four kinds of programme. These programmes *were* adopted as part of the curriculum of the school but it would be persistence in their use over a period of time that would establish how far staff were convinced that the final theory-to-practice conversion had been right. This test had yet to come.

Objective 2: To test the proposition that participation in such an exercise offers the best medium for in-service education of teachers.

There was no objective way of assessing how we, the staff, had been 'educated' by our own participation; there was no equivalent of a 'Teacher Car Test' to measure *our* progress. We believed that the exercise clearly provided opportunites for in-service education but what influenced the individual teacher's professional growth was the extent to which these opportunities were taken up. We already had Mills' (1967, *op. cit.*) definition to outline for us what factors were involved and we decided to measure our exercise against his definition, piece by piece. His definition bears repeating here. He saw the process as one that would enable teachers to 'become open to a wider variety of information; capable of pursuing a wider range of goals; versatile in producing new ideas, knowledge and techniques of value both to the group and to others; increasingly effective in exchanging things of value with others.'

So how did our exercise measure up to this?

1. '. . . to become open to a wider variety of information'
Opportunities
There were two years of regular formal and informal sessions. There was study of information from outside sources, books, articles, research documents and résumés of much of this material. There was information provided by inquiry and research within the school—analysis of current practices, tapes of children's and adult speech and test results. It was open to staff to react to all this information and bring their personal insights back to the general discussions for a kind of feed-back reinforcement. The exercise also provided opportunities to acquire information about the planning of change within a school.

Take-up
The initiators did participate in serious shared study of all these sources of new information. They were mainly responsible for the compilation and presentation of the information which came from within the school. It is probably a characteristic of innovatory movements that initial drive comes from one or two individuals who are led to attempt innovation by some personal motivating impulse. In our case Evans was concerned with the professional competency of the school of which he was Head, and Groarke, because of the nature of his task with the Special Class, had to be always seeking solutions outside the normal school curriculum which had already proved insufficient to meet the needs of the children he taught. They came together, with language development as common ground, seeing co-operation as a more fruitful process than individual action. So their incentive to seek out new information was strong because it came to them personally as well as through their position as members of a group.

For the rest of the staff, there was always the possibility that the concentration on language development was, as it were, one stage removed from what each one considered to be of primary concern to them. It was unlikely that the primary concern of eight individual teachers would coincide, at one time, with the primary concern of the initiators so in everything the initiators did there would always be an element of proselytizing. They were conscious of this element but were never sure how far it affected progress at any one time, or how far it influenced staff openness to new information as the exercise progressed. It was a fact that all teachers attended all the formal meetings and most teachers participated in most of the informal discussions. All teachers, too, read the four basic books and some teachers spent a great deal of time studying them and writing notes on them. It was felt that those teachers who really studied the books were more clearly aware of implications for classroom practice than were those who merely made a cursory reading. Certainly we all found sections of the books hard to understand.

Information, derived from examination of current practices, generated more interest than did the 'pure' research we read about, and principles arrived at through in-school studies were more readily absorbed than were principles arrived at through a study of principles. It appeared that only a minority of teachers derived more stimulus from personal study than from group discussion and it could be that instigation for the majority of teachers in general, will always come from the 'studious' minority.

2. '... to become capable of pursuing a wider range of goals...'
Opportunities

The efficient pursuit of an aim or goal is dependent on the ability, to specify its nature and the purpose, of the pursuer. Clarity of definition plus belief in the possibility of goal attainment will govern the degree of persistence shown. When teachers are asked about aims, or indeed engage in self-reflective formulation of aims, they often appear to offer differing definitions according to the situation where the discussion takes place. Keddie, in her article 'Classroom Knowledge' (1971) refers to the 'Educationist Context' and the 'Teacher Context' and she found evidence that individual teachers in the 'Educationist Context' offer support for aims that disappear or are modified in the 'Teacher Context'. This is not to suggest that teachers are hypocrites but to suggest that in reality there are two questions being asked rather than one: 'What are the aims of Education?' and 'What are the aims of your teaching?'

Honest response to the first question can be what we would call 'idealistic aims' and honest response to the second question would be what we would call 'actual aims'. This is no place to enter into a full blooded argument about the aims of education but we would argue that the 'actual' aims need to be no betrayal of the 'idealistic' but rather are the action-bound consequences of idealistic formulations. 'Idealistic' aims can be agreed to or supported but they do not have the substance on which action can be based. Take these examples of 'idealistic aims'.

'My chief aim is that each individual child in my care should become a well integrated, well adjusted human being'.

and

'Emotionally, a child is given the opportunity to work out his problems through play'.

and

'. . . to guide each generation of children into a full appreciation of our culture, to quicken their social and moral awareness'. (Taylor, *et al.*, 1972).

Amen, say we all. But *how* is all this to be done?

Concentration on the 'how' brings in more complications. Teachers might generally agree that their 'actual aim', their genuine concern, is for the development of oracy but general agreement at that level need not lead automatically to general agreement at the next (action) level. One teacher may rigorously attempt to inculcate oracy by encouraging the children to talk nicely and correctly with the right accent and intonation and by concentrating the children's attention on unusual and attractive words. Another teacher, still aiming for oracy, may have grasped the difference between 'immediate' and 'mediate' language demands and realised that the liguistic structures required in one situation may be different in kind to those required in another. For this second teacher the 'actual' aims, with respect to the development or oracy, of one teacher will seem quite inadequate and restricted. For a second teacher language has ceased to be merely a form of communication but has become in effect a form of human action requiring a high degree of control and flexibility to meet many changing situations. Although this second teacher will now work to a multiplicity of oracy goals he will be in a better position than the first teacher to produce an appropriate curriculum to achieve these goals because his understanding of them has been enhanced. Understanding at this level is what is meant, in the context of the exercise, by a 'wider range of goals'. Dissatisfaction is the precursor to goal evaluation. It is unlikely that a teacher who is content with current goals and practices will care to make an effort to change them. There must be a period of self-examination. The 'Why Bother' stage of our exercise provided this opportunity, and so did Stage 3, 'Examination of Current Practices'. But this was not the mere creation of dissatisfaction for its own sake, it was an attempt to arrive at a reasoned and informed dissatisfaction so that as the discrepancy between goals and achievement became more obvious, a willingness and determination to act would emerge to resolve the dissonance.

Our exercise also provided the same kind of opportunities for scrutinizing our own in-service educational goals.

Take-up
Certainly during the exercise, exposure to a wider range of goals took place and most, if not all participants, underwent a deepening of awareness and a shift in position. There was dissatisfaction, and this showed itself in a variety of ways. Sometimes we felt a cold disillusionment and one teacher confessed she felt all her previous years of teaching had been a waste of time. Other teachers reacted strongly against the exercise itself, handling the uncertainty with a show of scepticism and amused malice. It was fortunate at times like this that the exercise was not the brainchild of just one individual. Because there were two initiators, opposition could not be focused and so develop into personal backbiting. At such times the proselytizing role of the initiators had to be emphasized and this was made difficult because there was no clear way of telling whether the dissatisfaction arose from goal re-appraisal, from the methodology of the exercise or from some personal characteristics of the initiators. And, of course, the initiators themselves were not aloof from what was going on. They were as much participants as the rest of the staff and so were themselves experiencing the dissatisfactions of reappraisal. Also, for them, there were other sources of potential dissatisfaction. They not only shared in the general reappraisal of teaching and language development goals, but they also had to appraise their own role as initiators and, in Evans' case, his role as Head and leader of the exercise.

Our conclusion about all this would be that exposure to a wider range of goals is bound to produce dissatisfaction. There may be a point, and this will depend very much on the personality of the individual concerned, where too much dissatisfaction produces resistance and negative feedback. The crucial element appeared to be that we never found an acceptable way of engendering dissatisfaction (essential for change) that was not taken, at least in part, as some form of criticism of what a teacher was already doing. For some teachers this element remained a source of nagging irritation, right through the exercise, and we cannot be sure whether such a feeling is the inherent property of all reappraisal or merely a product of the exercise as it was conducted.

After the exercise was completed and the programmes had become part of the school curriculum, we noticed that some members of staff adjusted to the shock of reappraisal by rationalizing a return to their pre-exercise position. A few specific examples will illustrate what we mean.

Teachers, in discussion, would suggest that what we had discovered about language during the exercise was 'after all only common sense' and it was even suggested that we had all known it all along. Or it was suggested that all good teachers do what the programmes set out to do in their everyday teaching. There was clear indication in this kind of statement that there had not been any perception of wider goals. After all, if the exercise had proved anything, it was that we had *not* been 'teaching it right' before. This had been abundantly clear and it was the desire to 'teach it right' that resulted in the programmes. Our examination of current practices had shown that the then existing strategies were inadequate to meet new goals and our test results had highlighted new possibilities. That teachers were reverting to their previous stance could mean they were rejecting the wider range of goals the exercise had produced or they were resolving the resultant dissonance by returning to the more manageable unified goal concept they held before the exercise began.

Another interesting example of this was that of one teacher who spent a great deal of time and effort converting the language programmes into written exercises. This was completely against the whole meaning and purpose of the programmes. The very considerable strength of this teacher was his ability to create detailed written assignments so his attempt to convert speech programmes into written assignments was probably his particular way of reverting to his previous stance.

3. '... versatile in producing new ideas ...'
Opportunities
The exercise itself was, for the participants, a new idea and since a search failed to reveal any detailed record of a similar venture we

suggest it might well be a new idea as far as other teachers are con-cerned. Since what we were doing was new, there were no guidelines, so it was up to participants to provide all the ideas for the continuation of the exercise. It was also up to us, as participants, to extract ideas from the research and convert them into practices. This was especially true of Stages 6 and 9.

Take-up

Steiner (1965) has it that creativity is a characteristic of a small minority of people. We found that most teachers suggested elaborations or modifications of the exercise procedures and of the language pro-grammes from time to time, but the really dramatic insights and shifts of emphasis came almost exclusively from two people.

Our comments here relate only to the exercise. For a true measure of the effect of the exercise on versatility in producing new ideas it would be necessary to investigate how participation affected teacher performance in other areas of the curriculum. This would be a measure of whether the exercise had any real in-service educational effect.

4. '... producing new knowledge ...'

Opportunities

We have produced a great deal that is new.

We have produced a detailed record of the exercise. We have recorded evidence of teacher classroom practices and a great deal of recorded evidence of children's speech. This material is available for reference and study at any time. We have evidence that much of this material, and our interpretations of its value and meaning, is 'new' to teachers outside our own school, and it has been presented to others at several meetings.

Our programmes exist, the slides exist, the charts exist, the kits exist and the Teachers' Handbooks exist. They all exist and the programmes are very simple to operate.

These are the tangible products of our exercise.

Take-up

We can safely say that all of us have gained new knowledge from the exercise; knowledge about language development and knowledge about the nature of real in-service education. Each one of us has contributed something to this fund of common knowledge.

Interest in some of the material we produced was at a high level. This was especially true of the recordings and investigations we made of what the children actually said and did. This kind of objective

I

evidence is rarely available to teachers for the moment is quickly passed and the magical element we had, that of children actually participating in their teachers' in-service education, is the one so often missing at courses and conferences. What children actually do is what teachers are concerned about and when our exercise was concentrating on this area teachers operated best.

Certainly we can say that those members of staff who participated in our exercise will always be less ready than they were before to accept the ill-prepared, the vague, the irrelevant, the inexact and the shoddy as in-service education. This is basically the new knowledge they all have.

5. '... techniques of value ...'

Opportunities

What we did was new, we could unearth no guidelines from elsewhere, therefore we had to evolve our own techniques. The exercise itself, as a vehicle for curriculum innovation and as a medium for in-service education was our technique for coping with two separate needs within the school. It was of value to us and could be of value to others. The Model was the technique we used to control the progress of the exercise so that our energies would not be dissipated and we could see our way to a definite end product. Our model, or something similar, could be used as a basic management strategy in the handling of curriculum change.

We devised our own Test procedures. This was our technique for coping with the problem that faces all innovators—how can you be reasonably sure that the new will be better or more worthwhile than the old? We could have done this by collective subjective judgement but we all felt the need for something more specific than that. Although the test we produced was far from perfect, at least within our experience of constructing it, we gained first hand knowledge of the difficulties involved in making a good test. We also worried over all the techniques required for analysing any test results and had to find ways of presenting results clearly and logically.

We were totally unable, with our meagre training and intellectual and academic equipment to undertake studies of such complex matters as 'Loban's Weighted Scale' or Chomsky's model of transformational grammar. We had to simplify our approach to testing and even then we found difficulties.

The test involved two model cars, both of which were yellow and of similar size. One was a saloon and the other an open sports model.

Tania was asked, 'Which car do you like best?' In common with most of the children she said, pointing, 'That one.' To prevent pointing and to obtain verbal utterances, the children were asked to place their hands behind their back. This Tania did and then said 'That one,' attempting to indicate one of the cars with a form of eye-pointing. She then leaned forward and pointed with her nose!

'Which one, Tania, don't point'.
'The yellow one'.
'But they are both yellow'.
'Ummmm'.
'I don't know which one you mean'.
'I know'.
'Go on, tell me'.
'Both of them'.
'But which *one* do you like the best?'
'The yellow one'.
'But they are both yellow'.
'I like the yellow one'.
'And you can't tell me which one you mean. They are both yellow, you see'.
'I know, properly'.
'You tell me'.
'The yellow ones'.

In analysing the results, we had to classify Tania as 'unable' to differentiate, in words, between one car and the other. But, she scored highly in Total Verbal Output which we calculated on the basis of every word spoken during the test.

Mark, who in reply to the same test question said, 'The one with the flag' was 'able' in this section of the test while his brief but correct response increased his Total Verbal Output by only five words. The question, 'Tell me anything you like about this model' was badly phrased. Most children replied, 'I like the cars, I like the road, I like the policeman . . .' What the questioner meant was 'Tell me more about this model'. Definitely, a tape edited so that each child's first, second and third test recording appeared consecutively was of more interest to teachers than the pages of statistics and graphs which were produced.

The construction of the programmes involved the use of techniques for splitting up a basic pedagogical intention into small learning units. Once we had our units we had to devise techniques for teacher present- ation and our Teachers' Handbooks contain hundreds of references to these. As a by-product of all this, it was open to staff to learn something of the use of the camera for making slides and the use of the slide projector itself.

Above all, we found one answer to the major problem of converting theory and research into viable classroom practice.

Take-up
The value of these techniques, for ourselves as participants, depended on how appropriate they were for meeting the needs of the exercise and the extent to which each individual understood and shared in their making. Certainly, for us, they worked and we shall never know if better techniques could have been more effective. We, the initiators, are unhappy about the Car Test and would defend it only on the grounds that it was the best we could produce at the time. We learned a great deal from it and as a general affirmation that we were actually having a beneficial effect on the children's language development, we would still accept the results as valid.

Both as a way of bringing about genuine curriculum innovation in schools and as a way of in-service education for staff, we would still support the exercise as a viable mode of operation. We have many reservations about our own experience, but in terms of immediacy, relevance, genuine exposure of staff members to hard and critical thinking about their own practices and for converting what experts say into what children do, the exercise or something like it offers, we believe, sound possibilities. The Procedural Model we see as an integral part of any exercise, and unless the participants are very clear about where the exercise should go next, this should always be written down.

Our final evaluation of the 'take-up' of participants, in the area of valid techniques, comes again to the point about participation. The more actively involved participants were in the creation of the techniques, the more wide the knowledge and the more deep the understanding of them will be.

Because degree of participation appeared so crucial a factor in the efficacy of the exercise, especially in terms of in-service education, we attempted to investigate the many factors that affected it. This following section contains some of our observations.

Factors affecting participation
We tried to set a measure to participation by grouping it at four levels. These were:

Level One : Total involvement at all stages of the exercise, including the writing of the record.

Level Two : Participation in nearly all informal discussion; participation in all formal discussion, study of the four basic books together with all the prepared documents; AND making positive contributions to the planning, manufacturing and development of the programmes; making written notes at some stage of the exercise.

Level Three : Attendance at most discussions, formal and informal; reading one or more of the four books, completely or in part and reading some of the documents.

Level Four : Attendance at formal meetings.

We estimated that staff participated as follows:

Level One	2 teachers
Level Two	2 teachers
Level Three	4 teachers
Level Four	2 teachers

From our many discussions we found out that one major factor governing participatory levels was time. All participants, except the Head, had responsibility for the day-to-day running of a class. This point was made repeatedly and rightly so. No teacher could sit down and study the research while the children were there, so participation in the exercise had to be outside normal school hours. This demand on time has been widely recognized.

'Time in which teachers can plan and devise new units of work with experimental materials is essential; there seems to be few arrangements for the regular release of teachers for this purpose. The allocation of working time to curriculum development is still largely confined to teachers from schools who are taking part in the trial stages of national projects'. (Smith, 1971).

Time off, for a term or a year, is given to a minority of teachers wishing to follow a prescribed course in pursuit of a qualification, but no time off is given to the majority of teachers who may be experimenting in curriculum development with the children they actually teach. We realize that here we appear to be asking for two quite different things at the same time—time off for teachers and in-school education for teachers—but rather we are suggesting that the in-school day might be reorganized in such a way that in-service educational exercises might be an integral part of what goes on in school rather than an external adjunct to it.

What teachers do with their time when the children have gone home has always been considered a matter of individual responsibility. We found in our discussions that this was a sensitive area. Some teachers made reference to the effect that domestic responsibilities had on the amount of time available for participation in in-service educational projects. Naturally the bachelors and spinster members of the staff were aggrieved at the suggestion that marital status or parental responsibility was to be related to professional effort. There were serious issues involved here. If it was to be expected that teachers with heavy domestic work-loads could not be called on to give as much time to professional tasks as teachers with lighter responsibilities then it could be argued logically, that pay differentials and promotional opportunities should be built on to these expectancies. During the exercise it did not in fact work out that the level of domestic responsibility was related to commitment. So far as time given was concerned it seemed to be interest and personal inclination that were key factors.

There *was* conflict, voiced from time to time and revealed in attitudes, because members of staff felt that discussion of language development was pushing out other priorities and staff often felt slighted by the scant attention paid to other cherished curriculum objectives they were working towards with the children. Individuals resisted the exercise.

'The resistant figure is drawn as someone, generally, who conceives of himself as being acted upon rather than participant in the process of change. He is no longer upward mobile, he separates himself in the cocoon of education from changes in the competitive world outside. He may go through the motions of change but he is unlikely to internalise any alteration in the manner of his working.' (Pellegrin, 1965).

Our exercise showed that the upward mobile teacher can be equally resistant if he sees another's priorities are not for those areas that are currently enhancing promotional prospects. Resistance can also come from the teacher very strongly bound up to his own line in curriculum development, especially when he is working very much on his own.

What the exercise showed clearly was that, given a set exercise in curriculum innovation, what teachers contributed to it and what they got out of it depended not only on the strength of the mutual experience but also on their individual share in what was going on. Hoyle put this succinctly,

'Ultimately, the individual teacher is the "adopting unit" who will determine the effectiveness of an innovation and some teachers have more open minds than others as a function of their cognitive, perceptual and creative skills.' (Hoyle, 1971).

In-service education: alternatives to the exercise

It may appear to be stating the obvious to say that the value of any form of educational process depends on the cognitive, perceptual and creative skills of the participants. But recognition of this fact means that evaluation of in-service educational provision for teachers must be directed to discovering forms that best tap those personal attributes. Our stated Objective 2 was to find out if the exercise format was the best provision we could make for our own in-service education at the time, taking into account what was then on offer to us.

The main alternative on offer to us at the time was regular attendance at the local Teachers' Centre. Some of us had already rejected that alternative because, at best, sessions there consisted entirely of one-off lectures on a variety of unrelated topics or, at worst, chatty strolls down a nature trail or a couple of hours spent waiting for badgers to appear. Those who rejected these activities did not feel this kind of activity represented professional education. We are sure that our exercise, even for those teachers who participated at Level Four, was more productive in terms of professional growth.

We were also offered from time to time courses and conferences of one day's, several days' or a week-end's duration. Some of us had attended these functions. We had found them pleasant occasions but the amount of real educational substance gained from attendance was hardly of a kind to produce even small curriculum changes when we returned to school.

Another alternative that was always a possibility was that we might be seconded to attend a one-year full-time course. Obviously this could prove quite fruitful but the nagging question that such a course of action brought with it had to be—'Was it necessary to leave the children in order to learn better how to teach them?' Was an in-school exercise over a protracted period more beneficial for the children than one teacher attending a course away from them? And what about the in-service education of the teachers not seconded? It was interesting that Groarke, one of the initiators, did in fact attend a one-year course later on, when the exercise was completed, and the comparative value of the two forms of action concerned him. He was unable to give a definite answer but he puzzled over the question.

'You know whatever you do when you finish the course, the children you return to will all be one year older. Whether they would have benefited more if you had stayed with them is the question you no longer dare to ask'. (Groarke, 1974).

We are satisfied that over the period in question, for the teachers who participated and for the children whom we taught, our exercise represented the best opportunity for in-service education that was available to us. We believe this would be true for many other teachers in many other schools but we do not have the evidence to support that belief.

In Conclusion
'Some (innovators), Commenius for example, have accepted the discipline of translating their ideas into materials and methods. And some practitioners, Michael Sadler and Horace Mann for example, have dealt in ideas as well as practicalities. The curriculum development movement is at its best as the inheritor of this tradition. It means that ideas be translated into action, that educational thought should accept the discipline of practice, and practice the leaven of critical thinking.' (Stenhouse, 1973).

This, in a small way, was what the exercise attempted to do. If we were to some extent successful in meeting the objectives then the exercise approach to curriculum development might be worth organizing and institutionalizing as part of the structure of in-service education. Given a degree of interest from those whose titles suggest a source of expert guidance, some recognition for the effort involved, and the time in which to undertake those aspects of the exercise that cannot be pursued in the classroom in school hours, in-service education could become a visibly productive process.

Acknowledgements
The participants in the exercise were Gwyn John, Gill Cornish, Winn Squance, Myrtle Daniel, Barbara Tibble, Gill MacCormack, John Mortimer, David Barker. From other schools assistance was given by Joan Williams, Charles Heycock and Margaret Evans. The interest and

knowledge of Peter Stone, Chairman of the PTA was also of considerable assistance. We wish to thank the Chief Education Officer, J. G. Owen, for his encouragement and willingness to discuss the progress of the project from time to time, and to the LEA for supporting innovation by the provision of practical assistance.

References

BERIETER, C., and ENGLEMANN, S. (1966) *Teaching Disadvantaged Children in the Pre-School.* New York: Prentice Hall.

BERNSTEIN, B. (1970) 'A Critique of the Concept of Compensatory Education'. In Rubenstein, E. and Stoneman, C. (Eds.) *Education for Democracy.* Harmondsworth: Penguin.

EVANS, P., and GROARKE, M. (1974) 'Language for Learning: an infraschool Exercise in Curriculum Development with In-service Education'. Available for consultation from the Authors.

GAHAGAN, D. M., and G. A. (1970) *Talk Reform.* London:Routledge and Kegan Paul.

GROARKE, M. (1974) 'So you go to the University', *Teachers World*, 3rd May.

HOYLE, E. (1971) 'Planned change in Schools'. Paper read at meeting of British Association for the Advancement of Science.

HOYLE, E. (1971) 'How does the curriculum change, Part 2', *J. Curric. Studies*, 3, 2.

JOHNSON, M. (1969) 'The translation of curriculum into instruction', *J. Curric. Studies*, 1, 2.

KEDDIE, N. (1971) 'Classroom Knowledge'. In Young, M. F. D., *Knowledge and Control.* London: Collier MacMillan.

LAWTON, D. (1968) *Social Class, Language and Education.* London: Routledge and Kegan Paul.

LURIA, A. R., and YUDOVICH, F. (1971) *Speech and the Development of Mental Processes in the Child.* Harmondsworth: Penguin.

MILLS, T. M. (1967) *The Sociology of Small Groups.* New York: Prentice Hall.

OWEN, J. G. (1969) 'The Management of Educational Innovation'. Paper read at OECD Invitational Conference, Cambridge.

PELLAGRIN, R. J. (1966) *An Analysis of Sources and Processes of Innovation in Education.* Eugene, University of Oregon, Center for the Advanced Study of Educational Administration.

SMITH, M. P. (1971) 'Curriculum change at the local level', *J. Curric. Studies*, 3, 2, 158–162.

STEINER, G. A. (1965) *The Creative Organization.* Chicago: University of Chicago Press.

STENHOUSE, L. (1973) 'Innovation and stress', *Times Educ. Suppl.*, 19th January.

TAYLOR, P. H., EXON, G., and HOLLEY, B. J. (1972) *A Study of Nursery Education.*

PART III

CURRICULAR INFLUENCES

Tradition and Change in the Primary School Curriculum in Northern Ireland

P. T. McConnellogue (Stranmillis College of Education)

Introduction

Primary schools in Northern Ireland share many of the characteristics of their counterparts in England and Wales. Children begin at the same age, progress through classes based on age grouping, and transfer (via a selection procedure) to secondary education at 11+. Teachers are selected and educated in a similar way and work in the same variety of school buildings as their colleagues in Britain.

One fundamental difference between the systems is that what is taught in Northern Ireland's primary schools has traditionally been determined by a curriculum programme rather than by the schools themselves. This is a feature which Northern Ireland shares with Scotland, the Irish Republic and many other educational systems; that such programmes are not a feature of primary education in England and Wales makes this system unusual.

In recent years, the nature and functions of the 'primary programme' in Northern Ireland have changed to the extent that what was once a compulsory curriculum has now become an 'advisory curriculum' which 'embodies recommendations, no regulations and is not binding on schools' (Olsen, 1974). A similar change appears to be currently characteristic of other educational systems with originally compulsory curricula.

Whilst this shift in function is an interesting phenomenon in itself, it may present difficulties for the schools and teachers. It implies a break with their traditional role of implementors of a curriculum and now requires a changed role involving curriculum planning and development—a change with many ramifications for primary schooling.

141

This paper outlines the shift in function in the case of the Northern Ireland 'Programme for Primary Schools' and explores the effects of the change on the curriculum of a group of teachers, on what influences them in their work and on how they now feel the curriculum should be planned.

Evolution of the Programme

Beeby (1962, 1966) has offered 'an hypothesis of stages in the growth of a primary educational system' which is useful in identifying phases in the evolution of the curriculum. Based on the quality of education and training of the available teachers, he proposes a four-stage model of development:

(a) Dame school stage

Teachers are poorly educated with little or no professional training and the educational system is not organized but merely a collection of schools. In terms of curriculum there is no formal programme and what is taught reflects an emphasis on the 'three Rs' and on rote learning.

(b) Stage of formalism

Teachers are both educated and trained, but to a low level. The educational system has become highly organized with an official programme and prescribed texts which are rigidly adhered to and related to an external examination. Internally, the schools are organized to a rigid pattern, emphasis on the 'three Rs' continues along with rote learning but there may be an extension of the curriculum, normally to include history and geography.

(c) Stage of transition

Better educated and trained teachers promote a less formal classroom atmosphere. The official programme continues but is a good deal less rigid; prescribed texts and examinations also continue but there is a greater recognition of emotional and aesthetic values.

(d) Stage of meaning

Teachers are well educated and trained. The curriculum characteristics are a greater attention to the individual and a lessening of the importance of external controls, e.g. official syllabus, reduction of external examinations and less emphasis on inspection.

(i) Dame school and formal stages

Applying this to the Northern Ireland context, both the 'dame school' period and the period of 'formalism' had passed before Northern Ireland became a separate state. The dame school period is most closely paralleled by the Irish hedge schools of the 18th and 19th centuries, while the stage of formalism can be more precisely dated, between 1831, when a national system of education was founded in Ireland, and 1921, when Northern Ireland became a separate state. The content of curriculum during this period was defined by a set of textbooks produced by the Commissioners for Education which, although not compulsory (and not, therefore conforming to Beeby's characteristics), were used in almost all schools. These texts were essentially all-purpose primers which introduced the child to letter forms and simple words in Book 1 and ultimately to a broad curriculum including geography, natural history, reading skills, history, zoology and science (see Akenson, 1970).

This stage, while exhibiting the characteristics of Beeby's formalism, provided the basis for a much wider and more enlightened curriculum than was envisaged in his original framework. When the state of Northern Ireland came into existence, this appeared to coincide with the stage of transition in terms of the model under consideration. The next distinguishable period from 1932 to 1956 shares characteristics of both formal and transitional stages and is more accurately envisaged as an amalgam of both.

(ii) Formal—transitional stage—1932-56

The curriculum defined by the 1932 'Programme of Instruction for Elementary Schools' was more liberal (perhaps reflecting the inherited tradition) than the definition of elementary education contained in the 1923 Education Act which it operationalized, i.e. 'an education both literary and moral, based upon instruction in the reading and writing of the English language'. (This programme is summarized in Table 1.)

It applied to all schools, although a principal might implement a modified programme provided this was submitted to an inspector 'not later than the 1st May preceding the beginning of the school year'. Such tight control over what was taught was a characteristic of the 'stage of formalism'. The rigid organization of the school, i.e. after a period of infants, progression from Standards I to VII and the precise allocation of time to curriculum areas, also reflect this stage.

Control of the curriculum within the school was also tight, it being the responsibility of the principal to oversee the detailed schemes of

Table 1: Curriculum pattern: 1939–1956

Standard	Compulsory subjects		Optional subjects
Junior Infants	English Drawing Number Educational Handwork Songs and Games		
Senior Infants	English Arithmetic Singing Drawing Handwork		
I and II (approx. 8–9)	English (oral and written) Information and Observation Lessons Arithmetic Singing, Physical Training Drawing and options	}8–9 hours 4–5 hours 2½ hours 3 hours	Needlework Handwork
III and IV (9–10+)	English (oral and written) Geography or Information Observation Lessons Arithmetic Singing, Physical Training Drawing, Handwork and options	}8–9 hours 4–5 hours 2½ hours 3 hours	History Irish
V, VI, VII (11–14)	English, Geography Arithmetic Singing, Physical Training Hygiene and Temperance Drawing Needlework Domestic Economy Handwork, Horticulture or Nature Study or Elementary Science Options as time available	8–9 hours 4–5 hours }3 hours 1½ hours }2½ hours	Irish History French Algebra Geometry

work by teachers plus their weekly plans. An Elementary School Examination, in addition to general inspections at least every three years (on the basis of which teachers were graded from 'highly efficient' to 'not efficient' on a four point scale), reinforced the strong external control of what was taught. The effect of the latter system has been noted in a Programme Committee Report.

'It is not surprising that what was intended to be a teaching syllabus capable of modification ... came to be regarded as an examination syllabus from which any deviation, however promising or desirable, was hazardous.' (Programme Committee Report, 1956, p. 4.)

While these characteristics reflect a formal stage, some 'transitional' characteristics also need to be noted. The first is the width of the curriculum compared with that of Beeby's formal stage. Secondly, the precise rating of teachers indicated above was eliminated in 1936, although a 'highly efficient' rating remained until 1947.

Thirdly, the educational standards and training of teachers were quite high. Fourthly, there was a gradual movement away from this programme in the 1940s, even though it remained official until 1956—

'Teachers were able to see in true perspective the faults of the official programme and to take fuller notice of advances which had been made in educational theory in the last 25 years.' (Programme Committee, 1956, p. 5.)

These factors justify identifying this as an in-between stage of 'formal-transitional'. The actual transitional stage was reached in 1956 with the publication of a new programme. This was preceded by a White Paper of 1944 which spelt out wider aims for primary education:

'The aim of the schools should be not only to teach the essential skills—the three 'R's of former days—but also to train the hand as well as the mind, to encourage grace and freedom of movement and to give full scope to the development of self-reliance and originality' (Educational Reconstruction, 1944, p. 19).

It was also preceded by the 1947 Education Act which defined primary education as the stage from 5 to 11 + and by the establishment of a Programme Committee of teachers and inspectors in 1952 to carry out the revision as well as by the internal reorganization of schools into seven stages from Primary 1 to Primary 7.

(iii) Transitional stage: 1956—mid 1960s
The new 'Programme for Primary Schools' of 1956 took its stand squarely on the classic Hadow Report (1931) doctrine that 'the curriculum is to be thought of in terms of activities and experience rather than knowledge to be acquired and facts to be stored' which was quoted in the Programme's introduction. Much play is made of the new freedom and flexibility for teachers, although the need for yearly schemes of work and weekly lesson notes is stressed—and both of these were required on inspection occasions.

The curriculum which emerged (Table 2) was still fundamentally subject-based, justified by the revising Programme Committee (Report 1956) as a 'matter of convenience to accept the division of the curriculum into subjects', although teachers were alerted to the need to integrate. In addition, wider aims of primary education are stressed when teachers are encouraged to ponder 'what are my pupils capable of intellectually, artistically, spiritually, socially and in qualities of personality', thus reflecting a concern for emotional and aesthetic development.

Table 2: Curriculum pattern: 1956–mid 1960's

Standard	Compulsory subjects	Optional subjects
Primary 1–3 (5+–7+)	Physical Education, play	1½–2½ hours
	Free use of class resources inc. art handwork and nature study	3–5 hours
	Stories, poetry, music, dramatic work	2½ hours
	Basic skills, reading, writing, number	5–8 hours
Primary 4–7 (8–11+)	English and handwriting	8–9 hours
	Arithmetic	3½–4½ hours
	Geography	1–1½ hours History
	Nature Study	1–1½ hours Irish (from p. 5)
	Art, handwork, needlework	2½–3½ hours
	Physical education	1–2 hours

Source: *Programme for Primary Schools* (Northern Ireland) 1956.

Internal control of subjects by specification of year-by-year content disappeared, being replaced by 'memoranda giving a broad picture of the standards of achievement a child should normally have attained at appropriate stages in his course' (i.e. at P3 and at P7). While the changing conceptions of some subjects were reflected in changed titles (e.g Physical Training had become Physical Education etc.), the basic curriculum pattern had not greatly altered from the previous stage. The transitional characteristics are largely evidenced by a less rigid curriculum format and a greater concern for the aesthetic and emotional development of the individual.

(iv) Stage of meaning: mid 1960s
The origins of this phase are associated with a cluster of factors. Firstly, a change in the selection procedure in 1966 replaced the attainment tests in English and Arithmetic with the use of record cards. This was seen officially as removing a constraint from the primary curriculum . . .'

neither the teaching nor the organization need be so closely geared to the requirements of an examination in English or Arithmetic and this greater freedom will, it is hoped, result in increased diversity and flexibility in the conduct of the schools' (Report of the Minister of Education, 1965, p. 12).

Secondly, the initial curriculum development work of the Nuffield Foundation began to affect educational thinking in Northern Ireland, to the extent that, in 1966, a Ministry of Education circular drew teachers' attention to new developments in teaching mathematics and science, and schools were encouraged to develop new courses and syllabuses beyond what was included in the 1956 Programme.

Thirdly, recent reappraisals of primary education, in England by the Plowden Committee (1967) and in Wales by the Gittins Committee (1967), prompted a similar examination of primary education in Northern Ireland by the Advisory Council for Education (Northern Ireland). Though not primarily concerned with curriculum, the report, Primary Education in Northern Ireland, the Burges Report (1968), displayed some disenchantment with the 1956 programme.

'The intervening years have seen the introduction of fundamentally new approaches to the teaching of a number of subjects and have rendered this document largely out of date' (Burges Report, 1968, p. 49).

The report recommended that the 'programme' should be replaced by a 'guide' though it did not make explicit the distinction between these. The other important recommendations were the establishing of closer links with the Schools Council and the development of Teachers' Centres.

These three factors constitute the grounds for identifying a new stage of curriculum evolution in Northern Ireland. There is a distinct move towards 'child-centredness' in the Report, which comments that 'it is not too much to say that a beneficial revolution is occurring in primary teaching'. This is echoed in other documents: for example, the 1970 Report of the Ministry mentions that:

'Traditional timetable arrangements with separate subject divisions have been modified to allow for a more unified treatment of the curriculum and freer scope for the expression of the skills and interests of individual pupils' (Report of the Ministry of Education, 1970).

The abandonment of the official programme and a changing role for the inspectorate (towards advising) reflect the characteristic of a lessening of external controls.

While the establishment of teachers' centres has been piecemeal, the other recommendations of the Burges Report were acted on more quickly. In 1969 two groups, both broadly representative of educational interests, were established. One, the Primary Study Group (the equivalent of the earlier Programme Committee) has the responsibility of producing the new guide (not available at the time of this study). The other, the Northern Ireland Schools' Curriculum Committee, came into existence 'to advise the Ministry on Northern Ireland participation in Schools Council projects and on the dissemination of information about the Council's work' (1970 Report of the Ministry). This role is discharged by having observers at the Schools Council steering committees, by the publication of a 'News Bulletin' and by arranging for the participation of schools in Schools Council projects.

These developments appear to constitute another characteristic of the 'stage of meaning' not identified by Beeby (but noted by Hughes, 1969, in his examination of the Tasmanian curriculum), namely a proliferation of curriculum—associated bodies.

(v) Conclusion

The sequence of development in the formal curriculum of Northern Ireland primary schools, as it emerges from official documents and publications, follows a pattern close to, but not totally consistent with, Beeby's model. It displays the same overall sequence of development from tightly controlled uniform courses to a much more open primary curriculum situation, although this process is not smooth but goes in a series of spurts and halts.

Focusing the Study

(i) The process of change

The analysis of curriculum change outlined in the previous section suggests significant differences between the process of change in Northern Ireland and that in England and Wales. Hoyle (1973) has recently suggested that curriculum change proceeds through a number of more or less sequential stages, from diffusion (evolutionary as opposed to planned), a stage of research, development and dissemination (change mainly via curriculum development) a problem-centred phase, and a (yet hypothetical) professional-centred approach. Northern Ireland differs from this in being more reminiscent of countries with centrally defined curricula where change proceeds in cycles of 'programme—revision—programme'. More recently the system is showing signs of the research-development/dissemination model with school-based development, thus displaying characteristics of both types of educational system.

But if the process of change is different for both systems, the general direction of change is similar, that is towards a more child-oriented curriculum. What is uncertain is how far this change to a child-centred approach has taken place in practice in Northern Ireland on any widespread scale. Official reports and documents, clearly suggest a 'revolution' in primary education and a distinct move away from the curriculum of the last official programme.

Given, however, that Northern Ireland is an educational system traditionally controlled from the centre, reliance on the last available programme may still be considerable in the classroom. The 'revolution' may not in fact have taken place simply because of the tradition of expecting an outside body to provide a curriculum. Consequently, the residual effects of the curriculum programme on the structure and content of the day-to-day curriculum of the primary school is one area for investigation.

(ii) The teachers' role in curriculum planning
The process of change described in the previous section raises questions about teachers' views as to how the curriculum should be planned. In the analysis provided earlier the original role of the teacher vis-à-vis the curriculum during the 'formal-transitional' stage was essentially that of receiver. During the transitional stage the role contained an increased planning element since the year-by-year prescription was less precise, although the overall framework was still prescribed. During the current 'watershed' period between the last programme and the expected 'guide', the planning aspect of the teacher's role will continue to increase as external controls (inspection, examinations, etc.) continue to decrease.

Such freedom is at variance with the tradition of the system. During the course of the past 15 years, the traditional prop of the curriculum programme has been removed and teachers have been counselled to experiment in developing their own approaches and courses. Such rapid innovation may be counter-productive in a system with a tradition of a centrally defined curriculum and Nisbet's (1970) comments about Scottish teachers is relevant in this connection:

'Perhaps the Scottish educational pattern is too authoritarian at heart so that it is unrealistic to expect teachers to show initiative or to do anything other than wait for a strong lead from the centre.'

In other words, authoritarian systems may generate their own obstacles to change in promoting too heavy a reliance on central prescriptions; a reliance which cannot quickly be changed and may leave its mark in the teachers' desire to get back to the old system of central planning. Consequently, a second aspect for investigation in this study was teachers' views about centralized planning of the curriculum and alternatives to this.

(iii) Current influences on the curriculum

The development of the curriculum outlined earlier suggests one other important feature, namely a process of change during which the curriculum, originally defined by one major influence, is now potentially open to a considerable range of influences.

The curriculum of the 'formal-transitional' stage was defined almost totally by the 1932 programme. The third phase, that of 'meaning', saw an increase in the range of home-based influences (the various new bodies which came into existence) and potential influences from outside (Nuffield Foundation, Schools Council, etc.). In relation to the areas identified for investigation, i.e. the residual effect of the last programme on the structure and shape of the curriculum and on teachers' attitudes, it seems important to consider the question of how much direct influence this last programme continues to exert and how strong this is in relation to the other elements of the influence system. This formed the third area of investigation.

(iv) Methodology

On the basis of these areas, three questions were formulated for investigation:

(a) How far does the general structure of the current curriculum of primary schools show signs of the traditional programme format and how far are there indications of a change away from this?

(b) What influence does the curriculum programme continue to exert on the *de facto* curriculum in comparison with other and more recent influences?

(c) To what extent do teachers appear to favour a centrally devised programme of the traditional type?

These areas were investigated using a questionnaire which requested general background information about the teachers and schools involved and contained sections concerned with exploring each of these questions. One hundred and twenty-two teachers in 13 schools within a single urban-rural education authority in Northern Ireland completed the questionnaire. The schools were chosen to cover the range of size and school type and, in terms of curricular practice and organization, were felt to be typical of Northern Ireland primary schools on the basis of the author's experience of visiting schools as a college of education lecturer and on the advice of colleagues with similar experience. Each of the sections which follow deals in detail with an analysis of the responses of these teachers in relation to each of the questions identified.

The Present Curriculum

To examine the relationship between the programme and the present curriculum of primary schools, a comparison was made of the overall pattern of curriculum content in both cases.

This comparison was facilitated by resolving the general question of similarity into three sub-questions:

(a) to what extent is there evidence of the combination of traditional subjects? (structure);

(b) have new curriculum areas been added to the original core? (content);

(c) how far are time allocations to subjects comparable to the times suggested by the programme? (time).

Teachers were provided with a list of possible content areas and activities and asked to indicate those upon which time was spent by their class, and to estimate the approximate time so spent. To allow for omissions in the list of content, space was left to enable teachers to add areas which they felt had been overlooked.

This approach is based on the idea of a mainly subject-centred curriculum; in the event of this being an inadequate way of describing their curriculum (e.g. in an 'integrated day' situation), teachers were invited to ignore the framework and write a brief description of their own curriculum.

All teachers chose to use the framework provided, with modifications in the form of notes. From the original sample, 10 were excluded, two because of inadequate detail, the others being either non-teaching principals or teachers responsible for remedial groups or classes. The remainder (112) were considered from the point of view of structure, content and time allocation.

(i) Curriculum structure

The term 'structure' here refers to the organizational pattern of curriculum content. As indicated earlier, the 1956 Programme was basically subject-centred for the upper primary (P4–7) and organized into groups of subjects (e.g. basic skills, free activities, art and craft, etc.) for the lower primary (P1–3).

Returns for the P1–3 group failed to indicate any marked changes in the organizational pattern. Two teachers only out of 51 claimed that they tried to integrate their curriculum to such an extent that the provided framework was misleading. In all other cases, the indications of the notes given by teachers (e.g. combining dramatic work, stories and music or art activities into the 'free' activities time) had already been suggested by the Programme.

Of the 61 teachers in the P4–7 group, five noted that the framework (and consequently the picture of their curriculum and time allocations) was misleading because they tried to inegrate all of the subjects they taught. A larger group (20) provided clear indications of regrouping notably in the areas of history, geography, science, i.e. that these were 'not taught separately' or were 'combined into environmental studies' etc. The largest group (37) completed the framework as provided, gave no indication of its inadequacy nor indicated that any considerable degree of integration had taken place, except by occasional themes or projects. They appeared to be adhering to a basically subject-based curriculum.

Overall, these returns suggest minimal movement away from the 1956 primary programme. This view is reinforced, on one hand, by the very considerable number of teachers who could be quite precise about the time spent (even in four or five cases to providing the time in minutes), and, on the other, by the number of teachers with minor specialist responsibilities. The latter type of organization, in which teachers interchange according to capabilities and teach such subjects as music to several classes, is characteristic of a subject-based system.

(ii) Curriculum content

The data were examined secondly for curriculum content. For this analysis (and the subsequent time analysis) those seven teachers who indicated a considerable degree of integration were omitted, and the remainder analysed. The results are tabulated (Tables 3 and 4), grouped according to the frequency of mention of the areas in the framework, and of areas added by teachers.

In this instance indications of change away from the 1956 programme were taken to be additions to the traditional curriculum content or omissions from it.

It would appear that no additional discrete areas have been added by any substantial number of teachers. In the P1–3 group the items in the categories 'always' and 'generally included' correspond largely to the original areas of the programme (except for religious education, which was not, of course, prescribed). Items which might indicate additions fall into the 'seldom' or 'not included' categories.

Table 3: Content included in the curriculum by 49 teachers according to frequency of mention

(PRIMARY ONE–THREE)

Item No.	Description	N	Frequency of inclusion
4	Reading skills	49	
6	Mathematics	49	Always included
10	Music	49	100%
1	Story telling, poetry, etc.	48	
5	Free reading time	48	
18	Religious education	48	
25	Free activities	47	Generally included
3	Handwriting	46	75%
11	Art and craft	45	
7	Physical education	45	
2	Creative writing	44	
24	Radio and television	33	Frequently included 50%
19	Assembly	16	Occasionally included
16	Environmental studies	16	25%
26	Themes and topics	12	
8	Health education	9	
14	Geography	7	
13	History	5	
15	Science	5	
20	Moral education	3	Seldom included
21	Irish—Irish studies	3	
12	Needlework	2	
17	Social studies	2	
A*	Nature study	2	
22	French	1	
A*	Natural science	1	
23	Other languages	0	Not included
9	Sex education	0	

A*   Added by teachers to the original list.
Note: Categories (right hand column) give an indication of the percentage represented by N.

In P4–7 range, again, the 'always' and 'generally included' categories contain the basic programme prescription with the exception of nature study. Of the two originally optional subjects History and Irish, History is included by more than half the teachers, while Irish is included by only a small proportion of teachers in voluntary schools.

Table 4: Content included in the curriculum by 56 teachers according to frequency of mention

(PRIMIRY FOUR–SEVEN)

Item No.	Description	N	Frequency of inclusion
2	Creative writing	56	
6	Mathematics	56	Always included
18	Religious education	56	100%
11	Art and craft	53	
5	Free reading time	51	
1	Story telling, poetry, etc.	51	
7	Physical education	49	Generally included
4	Reading skills	49	75%
10	Music	45	
14	Geography	45	
24	Radio and television	40	
13	History	37	
26	Themes and topics	35	Frequently included
3	Handwriting	32	50%
12	Needlework	30	
19	Assembly	24	
16	Environmental studies	17	Occasionally included
15	Science	15	25%
25	Free activities	13	
21	Irish—Irish studies	8	
8	Health education	8	
22	French	7	
17	Social studies	5	
A*	Nature study	2	Seldom included
A*	Dictation	1	
A*	General English	1	
A*	11+ coaching	1	
A*	Road safety	1	
A*	Dictionary practice	1	
20	Moral education	1	
9	Sex education	1	
23	Other languages	0	Not included

A* Added by teachers to the original list.
Note: Categories (right hand column) give an indication of the percentage represented by N.

'Environmental studies', included by approximately one-third of the group is the only significant change. From the notes provided by teachers, most who include this understand it to be a combination of history, geography and, in some instances, science. This, therefore, represents more accurately a regrouping rather than an addition. As with the P1–3 group the appearance of potential additions to the curriculum in the 'seldom' or 'not included' categories suggests that there are no additions to the traditional curriculum by any significant number of teachers in the group.

Table 5: Time spent on curriculum areas compared with Programme recommendations

A. PRIMARY ONE–THREE   NUMBER OF TEACHERS—FORTY-NINE

Content	Items	TIME COMPARED WITH PROGRAMME			N (100%)
		Less	Same	More	
Physical education and movement	7, 8	22 49%	23 51%	0	45
Free activities, art, handwork, nature study	5, 11, 12, 15, 25, 26	16 33%	9 18%	24 49%	49
Stories, dramatic work, music	1, 10	8 16%	19 39%	22 45%	49
Reading, writing, number work	2, 3, 4, 6	0 —	22 45%	27 55%	49

B. PRIMARY FOUR–SEVEN   NUMBER OF TEACHERS—FIFTY-SIX

Content	Items	Less	Same	More	N (100%)
English and handwriting	1–5	15 27%	12 21%	29 52%	56
Arithmetic	6	10 18%	16 28%	30 54%	56
Geography	14	8 18%	31 68%	6 14%	45
Nature study (science)	15	5 29%	11 65%	1 6%	17
Music	10	2 4%	42 94%	1 2%	45
Art, handwork, needlework	11, 12	27 52%	13 24%	13 24%	53
Physical education	7	5 10%	44 90%	0	49

(iii) Time

The data contained in this section were examined finally in relation to the time indicated for each aspect of curriculum, since a characteristic of the programmes was the indication of upper and lower limits of time for each subject.

Two adjustments to the data were necessary before this examination could be undertaken. The time being spent by teachers on radio and television programmes, in cases where this was not already included in the time allocation, had to be calculated and reapportioned to the relevant curriculum area. With the help of notes included and the indication of programmes used this was possible in all but seven cases. (In these cases insufficient data regarding programmes were provided and the basic time given by teachers was taken as the total time). Secondly, for purposes of comparison with the Programme, it was necessary to reorganize the subjects according to the Programme format.

On this basis teachers were grouped according to whether they spent more, less, or approximately the same time as the Programme prescription (Table 5). In some instances, e.g. English and Mathematics (P4–7) a substantial proportion of teachers now spend more time on these areas than originally suggested. There is some suggestion that some subjects peripheral to the basic skills curriculum (nature study or natural science, art, etc. for P4–7) have lost ground compared to the original time suggestion. Overall it remains difficult to say clearly the extent to which the Programme prescription still forms the basis of time allocation, but it is notable that in three widely included areas (physical education, geography, music in P4–7 range) a very high percentage of teachers make a similar allocation of time to that given in the programme.

(iv) Conclusion
Teachers' perceptions of their transactional curriculum suggest that the everyday curriculum is closer to that outlined by the 1956 Programme than to the radically changed one hinted at in official documents, and that the Burges Report's (1968) use of the term 'revolution' hardly characterizes what change there has been.

Curriculum Influences
The most comprehensive attempt to identify an influence system and its internal strengths and structures appears to have been that used in a study of English primary schools as part of the Schools Council 'Aims of Primary Education Project' (Taylor, Reid, Holley and Exon, 1974). This approach appeared to offer the most useful way of understanding the Northern Ireland situation and was used in this instance.

The original list of influences was modified to suit the N. Ireland context, giving 31 possible influences which teachers were asked to rate according to the extent to which they felt, firstly, the school curriculum and, secondly, the class curriculum were influenced by them. As in the original study, teachers were also asked to indicate how far they felt they could reciprocate each influence; this section was retained not merely for comparison but also because it appeared to offer a way of gauging the extent to which teachers felt they could affect traditional authoritarian influences.

(i) School influence system
Teachers' ratings of the perceived strengths of the influences were tabulated by means and standard deviations (Table 6). Eight sources

Table 6: School influences: group mean rating

Item	Description	Mean	SD	Degree of Influence
11	Principal	3·36	1·27	
2	Colleagues	3·10	0·96	
9	HMI	2·75	1·02	
22	Formal staff meeting	2·74	1·34	Definite influence
25	Ministry of Education*	2·61	1·20	2·5
15	'Programme of Primary Schools'	2·61	1·09	
8	Informal group of staff	2·57	1·11	
17	Teacher (self)	2·55	1·25	
14	Pupils	2·48	1·13	
10	National media	2·39	1·08	
26	Local education authority	2·27	1·11	
4	Vice-principal	2·27	1·16	
24	Local reports	2·21	0·90	
6	Nuffield, Schools Co., etc.	2·17	0·97	
29	Professional visitors	2·16	0·95	
7	LEA advisers	2·15	1·08	
23	Textbook company	2·13	0·93	
16	National reports	2·07	0·95	
13	Parents	2·06	0·98	Of little influence
3	College, university	2·01	0·93	1·5
1	Professional journals	2·00	0·81	
5	Northern Ireland Schools Curriculum Committee	1·93	1·01	
18	Educational writers	1·91	0·79	
31	Colleagues in other schools	1·85	0·85	
20	Teachers centre	1·84	1·05	
19	Chief education officer	1·78	0·91	
30	Local teacher group	1·70	0·83	
21	NFER	1·51	0·72	
27	National educational associations	1·50	0·74	
12	Northern Ireland Council for Educational Research	1·49	0·76	Of minimal influence
28	House of Commons	1·21	0·61	0·5

* Since this study was completed, the 'Ministry' has been renamed the 'Department of Education' and local education authorities have been replaced by 'area boards'.

appear to exert a 'definite' influence (i.e. an influence greater than the mean of 2·5) on the school curriculum. It is notable that these influences represent a mix of both 'within school' category influences and the regional influences and, more particularly, that those in the latter category (HMI, 'Programme', Ministry of Education) are all influences from the central controlling body of education. They are, moreover, influences of a traditional nature in the sense that they have always existed in the system. More recent sources of influence which also emanate from the centre (e.g. Northern Ireland Schools Curriculum Committee) exert a good deal less influence. Most members of the 'within school' group exert a definite influence, with the notable exception of the vice-principal. Pupils fall just outside the 'definite' influence rating, while parents appear to exert 'little' influence. The least influential of the regional influences is the Northern Ireland Council for Educational Research, perhaps due partly to teachers' lack of interest in research as well as to the fact that this body to date has sponsored relatively little research in the primary sector.

The 'within school' category and the regional influences seem, therefore, to be the most influential groupings and this is further indicated if the influences are grouped according to type and origin and the means of these categories examined (Table 7).

Table 7: Categories of influence by mean score

Category	Items	Mean Score
Educational National	1, 6, 16, 18, 21, 23, 27	1·91
Educational Regional	3, 5, 7, 9, 12, 15, 19, 20, 24, 25, 26, 29, 30, 31	2·13
Within School	2, 4, 8, 11, 14, 17, 22	2·72
Lay National	10, 28	1·80
Lay Regional	13	2·06

(ii) Classroom influence system

As in the English study, a different influence system appears in this context to operate on the classroom (Table 8). The class teacher has the greatest power to influence (the only source within all categories which can be classified as a 'strong' influence). The remainder of those capable of exerting a marked influence on the classroom are drawn from the 'within school' category. Nevertheless, the inspectorate and the 'Programme', both centrally based influences, are only marginally less strong.

Formal staff meetings, the deputy principal, advisers and parents appear to have less capacity to influence the classroom than the school. Pupils and educational writers, on the other hand, have more influence on the classroom, suggesting, perhaps that teachers perceive themselves as more open to influence from their immediate clients and from educational literature (though not from professional journals). In general, however, the classroom influence system is dominated by fewer and more definite influences than the school as a whole.

(iii) Reciprocation of influences

The influence sources most easily reciprocated by the teachers themselves are those physically closest, the 'within school' group (Table 9).

Table 8: Classroom influences: grouped mean ratings

Item	Description	Mean	SD	Degree of Influence
17	Teacher (self)	4·32	0·95	Strong influence 3·5
11	Principal	2·70	1·19	Definite influence
14	Pupils	2·69	1·16	2·5
2	Colleagues	2·56	0·96	
9	HMI	2·49	1·03	
15	'Programme for Primary Schools'	2·48	1·08	
8	Informal group of staff	2·48	1·06	
10	National media	2·44	1·14	
22	Formal staff meeting	2·44	1·25	
25	Ministry of Education	2·38	1·14	
18	Educational writers	2·16	1·06	
23	Textbook company	2·07	0·98	
6	Nuffield, Schools Co., etc.	2·07	0·91	
16	National reports	2·07	0·92	
24	Local reports	2·06	0·90	
26	Local education authority	2·05	1·05	Of little influence
29	Professional visitors	2·05	0·94	1·5
31	Colleagues in other schools	2·04	0·93	
3	College, university	1·97	0·88	
13	Parents	1·94	0·92	
1	Professional journals	1·93	0·81	
7	LEA advisers	1·84	0·88	
4	Vice-principal	1·80	1·03	
5	Northern Ireland Schools Curriculum Committee	1·79	0·89	
20	Teachers centre	1·73	1·03	
30	Local teachers group	1·62	0·81	
19	Chief education officer	1·49	0·78	
21	NFER	1·48	0·69	
27	National educational associations	1·44	0·73	Of minimal
12	Northern Ireland Council for Educational Research	1·39	0·67	influence 0·5
28	House of Commons	1·14	0·43	

Again the position of the vice-principal is curious because he alone of these is less readily influenced than outside sources such as parents or colleagues in other schools. It is notable that some influences, notably the Ministry of Education, have power to influence out of proportion to their susceptibility to being influenced. The relative remoteness in reciprocation terms of some 'Educational Regional' sources, such as the Northern Ireland Schools Curriculum Committee, is also noteworthy when compared to the possibility of reciprocating national sources, e.g. Nuffield, National Press, etc. The general picture which emerges is that of a group of teachers which sees itself capable of reciprocating most of the influences to which it itself is subject.

Table 9: Reciprocation of Influence

Item	Description	N	Degree of reciprocation
2	Colleagues	108	Strong reciprocation
8	Informal staff group	95	80%
11	Principal	85	
22	Formal staff meeting	82	
14	Pupils	78	Considerable reciprocation
13	Parents	76	60%
31	Colleagues in other schools	72	
4	Vice-principal	69	Definite reciprocation
29	Professional visitors	60	40%
9	HMI	59	
30	Local teachers groups	46	
20	Teachers' centre	45	
3	Local college/university	44	
7	LEA advisers	40	
10	National press, etc.	30	Some reciprocation
1	Professional journals	34	20%
23	Textbook company	27	
6	Nuffield, Schools Council	25	
25	Ministry of Education	24	
15	'Programme for Primary Schools'	24	
26	LEA	23	
5	Northern Ireland Schools Curriculum Committee	22	
19	Chief education officer	20	
18	Educational writers	20	
16	National reports	18	Little reciprocation
24	Local reports	17	
12	Northern Ireland Council for Educational Research	15	
27	National educational associations	14	
21	NFER	11	
28	House of Commons	8	
			No reciprocation

Note: N=the number of teachers indicating reciprocation of influences. Categories are based on percentages of 118 respondents to this section.

(iv) Comparison of English and Irish teachers

It has been implied throughout this study that the English and Northern Ireland systems have different curriculum traditions and that the concept of a 'programme' is fundamental to one tradition and not the other. It has further been suggested that such a programme is an important factor in promoting an authoritarian tradition in which schools and teachers look to the centre for guidance. How far is there evidence of such differences?

Comparison with the study referred to earlier (Taylor *et al.*, 1974) suggests an overall pattern common to both systems. The influence of principal and class teacher respectively are paralleled in both systems, as is the general strength of the 'within school' group. The pattern of a more specific set of influences on the classroom than on the school also reappears in this study.

Some differences do exist between the groups. None of the educational reports, national or regional appear to be as influential on the Northern Ireland teachers as on their English counterparts. On the other hand the influence of the textbook company on both school and classroom is higher in Northern Ireland than in the English context. These differences are difficult to account for but may suggest a greater reliance by Irish teachers on texts, i.e. on a specific curriculum prop, which might be in keeping with a traditional reliance on a programme.

A more marked difference is the higher rating in the Northern Ireland system of influences associated with the central controlling body. These (Inspectorate, Ministry, Programme) rate almost as highly as the 'within school' group and this level of rating provides some confirmation of the authoritarian nature of the system.

It is difficult to compare the sections dealing with the reciprocation of influences because of what appears to be a low reaction rate in the case of the English study—as the authors comment. . . .

'it must be admitted that the data on reciprocation needs the amplification which would come from a more detailed study'.

(v) Conclusions

It seems clear that the 'Programme for Primary Schools' constitutes a definite influence on the school and a somewhat less strong influence on the classroom. It further makes clear that this influence is stronger than any of the more recent influences which have developed within the system, either at national level (e.g. Nuffield Foundation, etc.) or at regional level (e.g., LEA advisers, teachers' centres, etc.).

This is significant for a number of reasons. The last section suggested that the *de facto* curriculum appears to retain its major traditional characteristics which derived from the primary programme. The fact that so many teachers acknowledge the influence of the Programme provides support for this view. Secondly, the strong rating of centrally-derived influences further supports the view that the Northern Ireland system is centrally-oriented, i.e. expecting guidance from central authority. Thirdly, the rating of the programme (and indeed of the influence of the Inspectorate) points to the slow rate of decay of

L

traditional influences, even when change in the role and impact of these is desired and supported by the Ministry of Education and by official reports.

Who Should Plan the Curriculum?

This aspect of the study was based on Beauchamp's (1968) use of the concept of 'arena' for curriculum planning or 'engineering', which, in his analysis of curriculum systems, implies the level at which

'. . . all of the activities (planning, implementation and evaluation) inherent in a system of curriculum engineering . . . takes place' (page 18).

Beauchamp suggests that

'. . . the most obvious arena choices are the individual school, the school district, the state and the nation' (page 17).

In some systems no single arena exists, and Beauchamp argues that in centralized educational systems (France, Italy, etc.) a 'split function' system operates whereby the areana for planning is national but the arena for implementation is the school.

Applying this analysis to the Northern Ireland situation, three arenas were investigated, the region, the school and the classroom. In addition, to arenas, however, different types of personnel might have major planning roles (e.g. teachers and pupils in the classroom arena, assistant teachers and principal teachers at the school level). Consequently it seemed useful to explore the role of some of these agents in curriculum planning. A short section of eight items was eventually used (Table 11) covering the following arenas and agents:

Table 10: Curriculum planning arenas

Item	
1	Classroom arena, curriculum mainly determined by children
4	Classroom arena, curriculum mainly determined by teacher
7	Classroom/school overlap, curriculum planned by teacher and principal
5	School arena, curriculum planned by staff and principal
2	School arena, curriculum planned by principal
6	School/regional arena, curriculum planned mainly at regional arena
8	School/regional arena, curriculum planned mainly within the school
3	Regional arena, planning at regional level, implementation at school level

Table 11: Responses of teachers to various approaches to curriculum planning

				Distribution of responses				
No.	*Item*	*Mean*	*SD*	*1*	*2*	*3*	*4*	*5*
1	Children should be free to choose topics and activities which interest them, while the teachers help and encourage them in what they wish to do.	3·32	1·05	5	24	34	45	14
2	The school principal should plan the curriculum for each class in each subject area.	1·95	0·93	41	58	14	6	3
3	All schools and classes should follow a uniform curriculum, formulated by a central body which specifies areas of content to be taught and approximate amounts of time to be devoted to each area.	2·15	1·17	42	46	15	12	7
4	Individual class teachers should plan their own curriculum deciding the content and method most appropriate to their class.	3·48	1·25	8	27	13	46	28
5	The curriculum for a school should be planned by the teachers in the school in conjunction with the principal.	4·09	0·98	2	6	23	39	52
6	There should be a uniform centrally-devised curriculum for all primary schools which may be either followed by schools or modified by principals and their staffs to meet the local circumstances of the school.	3·75	1·04	2	15	27	45	33
7	Individual teachers should plan the curriculum for their own class in consultation with the principal.	3·26	1·04	4	32	24	52	10
8	There should be an official guide issued by the central authority responsible for education which discusses the principles upon which the curriculum might be based, but does not define content or method for each class.	3·80	0·91	3	8	23	65	23

KEY: 1 = strongly disagree; 2 = disagree; 3 = neither agree nor disagree; 4 = agree; 5 = strongly agree

Teachers were asked to rate each item on a five-point scale, indicating their agreement with the item, a rating of five being 'strongly agree' and of one, 'strongly disagree'.

A summary of teachers' responses to the eight items is given in Table 11. All items were positive statements varying along the 'agree/disagree' dimension. Taken overall, the responses suggest that teachers see the school as the major arena, with some degree of overlap with the regional arena. There are some differences between items which need to be considered more carefully.

Two approaches to curriculum planning clearly find little favour with teachers, that in which the principal is the main planner (item 2) and the traditional approach whereby a rigid curriculum is defined outside the school and implemented within it (item 3). Both of these situations are consistent with the approach to be found during a 'formal transitional' stage where schools implemented an externally determined curriculum to which modifications could only be made at the principal's discretion and for which he gave sufficient notice to the Inspectorate.

There is more support for the classroom as a planning arena (items 1 and 4), although teachers are not agreed about this, as indicated by the relatively high standard deviations on both items. It is also noteworthy that, while there is sympathy for children's freedom in activities (item 1), responses tend to favour the teacher as the main controlling agent in the situation, judged from the greater number of 'strongly agree' responses to item 4, despite an almost equal number of 'agree' responses. This is consistent with the strong influence the teacher sees himself as exerting in the classroom compared to that of his pupils (discussed earlier) and is supported by the findings elsewhere on teachers' views about 'child centredness' in the curriculum, in which the researchers concluded that

'. . . teachers see for themselves a very positive role in relation to the learning and motivation of the children they teach. For the teachers, self directed activity by the child is acceptable only within the limits ordered by the teacher'. (Taylor *et al.*, 1974, p. 58).

There does not, however, appear to be overwhelming support for a situation in which the classroom arena has a high degree of autonomy (item 4). Approximately half the teachers agree that the class teacher should have reference to the principal in this planning (item 7). This is consistent with the rating of the principal as the second most significant influence in the classroom, as discussed earlier.

Some form of outside help or guidance in the formulation of the schools curriculum would find general acceptance (items 6, 8). This implies some Ministry backed curriculum at a regional arena level. Item 6 was framed to reflect the situation of the 'Programme for Primary Schools (1956)', i.e. the situation characteristic of a 'transitional' stage. Although now outmoded in terms of current development the approach still finds favour with many teachers. Clearly, however, teachers are more in favour of the looser prescription of the type now in preparation as a 'guide' (item 8) both in terms of general support and of higher agreement (0·91 is the lowest SD of all the items).

The single approach to curriculum planning which receives most support is the situation in which the school staff as a whole engage in the planning activity (item 5), again both in terms of general support and of agreement (0·98 can be considered to reflect high agreement). What should be taught in schools, it appears, should be decided mainly within the school, which, again, is consistent with the picture suggested in the influence analysis, wherein the in-school group had very considerable power to influence.

(iv) Conclusions
Overall, teachers appear to favour a corporate planning procedure within the arena of the school, a situation in which no specific agent predominates in the planning. This marks a change away from the traditional classroom isolation of the Northern Ireland primary teacher. Help from outside the school from the regional arena appears to be desirable either in the form of a modifiable curriculum or of a guide. Teachers appear ambivalent towards the centrality of the third possible arena for planning, namely the classroom; items referring to this (1, 4, 7) have means close to the neutral 'neither agree nor disagree' and standard deviations greater than 1.

This analysis suggests a distinct change in the arena pattern. Between the classic 'split function' model of earlier stages of Northern Ireland development, with a regional planning arena and a classroom implementation arena, the school now emerges as a distinct and important planning arena in its own right, whereas the regional arena now develops into more of an auxiliary rather than a main planning arena. Teachers appear to accept a 'planning' role rather than a 'receiving' role in relation to curriculum, provided that this role can be accepted as a group and not as an individual one. Finally, the responses and the suggested development that these imply indicate that the move to develop a 'guide' rather than produce a new structured Programme appears to be the appropriate sort of support that schools and teachers require from the regional arena, such support now replacing the earlier dependence and reliance on the central authority.

Conclusions

The following broad conclusions may be tentatively drawn from the study of a sample of primary schools in Northern Ireland.

1. The curriculum framework traditionally legitimated by the 'Programme' appears to operate in most of these schools with relatively little change in terms of restructuring or additions.

2. The primary schools appear to be susceptible to two major types of influence, those of the school-based group and those of the Ministry of Education.

3. The predominant influence of the teacher in the classroom and the head in the school, suggested in the English study, is supported here.

4. Curriculum influences of a more recent origin exert relatively little influence on the schools.

5. Teachers display a preference for a curriculum planning process whereby major decisions on curriculum are taken on a co-operative basis within the school.

6. There appears to be a desire for broad over-arching guidelines legitimized by the Ministry of Education within which the above type of planning may take place.

In a transitional stage such as primary education in Northern Ireland has now reached, two factors seem particularly important—firstly, teachers' acceptance of such a transition, and, secondly, the development of adequate support systems which will ease the transition from a teaching role in which the curriculum is mainly 'given' to one in which it is created by the teachers, at least within certain limits. Regarding the first, the analysis of teachers' views about curriculum planning suggests that such an 'advisory curriculum' would find favour with teachers. There is no very strong evidence, therefore, that teachers' attitudes towards planning are so strongly affected by the tradition of the system that they insist on the traditional highly structured type of programme.

In the instance of support systems the situation is less optimistic. The analysis of influences suggests that the existing support systems (Northern Ireland Schools Curriculum Committee, teachers' centres, advisory services, Schools Council, etc.) exert little influence. Those influences which are important (Ministry, Inspectorate, etc.) are currently concerned with changing their role to one of less direct influence on the schools. This presents a rather confusing picture wherein those whose influence is acknowledged by teachers wish to exert less influence, while those sources who wish to influence teachers, and to offer support regarding curriculum change are finding it hard to do this. Thus, the difficulties of promoting school based curriculum change in Northern Ireland may be considerable unless the support systems, which now appear inadequate, are developed, strengthened and better co-ordinated. This does not imply central control but it does suggest more centrally based co-ordination of support until schools develop enough power as institutions to generate their own curriculum change.

For the schools, tradition appears to continue to play a major part in defining the operational curriculum. Viewed in Bernstein's (1971) terms there is little evidence of a move from a 'collection' to an 'integrated' type of curriculum code. Bernstein (1967, 1971) has argued that such a shift in curriculum structure is likely to be accompanied by changes in teacher's work relationships:

'. . . the integrated code will require teachers to enter into social relationships with each other which will arise not simply out of non-task areas but out of a shared, co-operative educational task. The centre of gravity of the relationships between teachers will undergo a radical shift . . . the administration and specific acts of teaching are likely to shift from the relative invisibility to visibility' (page 62).

The sort of institution which these schools portray (through the analysis of influences) suggests that the classroom is still a distinct and very autonomous arena. There is relatively little evidence of a *de facto* move towards either the 'teacher-based' or 'teachers-based' type of integration, although such a change in relationships as Bernstein discusses would be implied by the type of corporate planning which teachers seem to prefer.

Bernstein has suggested that 'Scotland is nearer to the European version of the collection code' (p. 53). It has been pointed out earlier that Northern Ireland and Scotland have much in common and it seems reasonable to identify clear links between these systems and continental systems in relation to both control of the curriculum and its coding, and to point to the English system as exceptional. His view that collection codes are highly resistant to change is supported in this study and Bernstein's verdict regarding integrated codes in an international context seems particularly applicable to Northern Ireland:

'It is probably true to say that the code, at the moment exists at the level of ideology and theory with only a small number of schools and educational agencies attempting to institutionalise it with any seriousness' (page 59).

Finally, in the general context of curriculum studies, this paper may help to focus on curriculum programmes as significant documents in a sociology of curriculum, concerned not only with how knowledge is organized and made available in schools (of which programmes are a formal statement), but also with the influences which shape curricula. In the study of these influences, curriculum programmes may act as devices which screen out some and focus on others.

References

Official documents and reports
ADVISORY COUNCIL FOR EDUCATION (Northern Ireland) (1968), *Primary Education in Northern Ireland*, (Burges Report). Belfast: HMSO.
CENTRAL ADVISORY COUNCIL FOR EDUCATION (England) (1967), *Children and their Primary Schools* (Vol. 1). London: HMSO.
CENTRAL ADVISORY COUNCIL FOR EDUCATION (Wales) (1967), *Primary Education in Wales*, (Gittins Report). London: HMSO.
CONSULTATIVE COMMITTEE OF THE BOARD OF EDUCATION (1931), *The Primary School*, (Hadow Report). London: HMSO.
MINISTRY OF EDUCATION (Northern Ireland) (all publications). Belfast: HMSO.—
1923, *Education Act (Northern Ireland)*.
1944, *Educational Reconstruction in Northern Ireland* (Cmd. 226).
1947, *Education Act (Northern Ireland)*.
1952, *Programme of Instruction for Elementary Schools*, (1932) (reprint).
1956, *Report of the Primary Schools Programme Committee*.
1956, *Programme for Primary Schools*
1966, *Education in Northern Ireland in 1965: Report of the Ministry of Education* (Cmd. 492).

Books and articles
AKENSON, D. H. (1970) *The Irish Education Experiment: The National Systems of Education in the 19th Century*. London: Routledge and Kegan Paul.
BEAUCHAMP, G. A. (1968) *Curriculum Theory* (second edition). Wilmette, Illinois: The Kegg Press.
BEEBY, C. (1962) 'Stages in the Growth of a Primary Educational System', *Comparative Education Review*, Vol. 6.
BEEBY, C. E. (1966) *The Quality of Education in Developing Countries*. Cambridge, Mass.: Harvard University Press.
BERNSTEIN, B. (1967) 'Open schools, open society', *New Society*, 14 September, 1967.

BERNSTEIN, B. (1971) 'On the Classification and Framing of Educational Knowledge'. In Bernstein, B. (1971) *Class, Codes and Control*. London: Routledge and Kegan Paul.

HOYLE, E. (1973) 'Strategies of Curriculum Change'. In Watkins, R. (Ed.) *In-service Training: Structure and Content*. London: Ward Lock Educational.

HUGHES, P. W. (1969) 'Changes in Primary Curriculum in Tasmania', *The Australian Journal of Education*, Vol. 13, 1969, p. 130 ff.

McCONNELLOGUE, P. (1974) 'The historical development and present influence of the Northern Ireland "programme for primary schools".' Unpublished. MEd dissertation, University of Birmingham.

NISBET, J. (1970) 'Curriculum Development in Scotland'. In Hooper, R. (Ed.) *The Curriculum: Context Design and Development*. Edinburgh: Oliver and Boyd.

OLSEN, T. P. (1974) 'Curriculum—its meaning and use in Denmark'. In Taylor, P. H., and Johnson, M. (Eds.) (1974) *Curriculum Development—A Comparative Study*. Slough: NFER.

TAYLOR, P. H., REID, W. A., HOLLEY, B. J., and EXON, G. (1974) *Purpose, Power and Constraint in the Primary School Curriculum*. London: MacMillan for the Schools Council.

This article was based on an unpublished M.Ed dissertation: McConnellogue, P. (1974) 'The Historical Development and Present Influence of the Northern Ireland "Programme for Primary Schools" ', School of Education, University of Birmingham.

A Study of the Curricular Influences in a Mid-Western Elementary School System

P. H. Taylor (University of Birmingham)

Introduction

The term 'curricular influence' has been employed in a number of empirical studies and refers to the forces, both social and ideological, which shape what is taught in educational institutions (Taylor and Reid, 1971; Taylor, Reid, Holley and Exon, 1974; Taylor, Reid and Holley, 1974; Taylor and Adams, 1974 and Taylor, 1974). The focus of interest has been on what *is* taught, on the *de facto* or operational curriculum, not on what *should* be taught. The aim of the studies has been twofold: to suggest where the power to influence what is taught resides and to describe the structure, form and character of the influence as distinctive sub-systems of influence. Additionally, the studies have taken the opportunity to relate influence to personal, institutional and ecological variables, and in some cases to explore the weight and shape of the constraints which inhibit the achievement of curricular aims.

'Influence', Parsons (1963) states, 'is an intangible property of relationships between persons and is concerned with . . . intentional attempts to bring about results.' The influence brought to bear on what the elementary school teaches and what is taught in its classrooms is concerned to achieve the intentions embodied in the school's programme which are shaped in practice by what is taught. Many individuals, organizations and agencies both locally and nationally have an interest in influencing the nature of these intentions, in shaping the everyday educational experience provided by the elementary school.

This study focuses on 28 such influences drawn from both the local and national educational scene, and from such local and national social influences as parents, Congress, the church and press, radio, TV and other mass media. In addition the influence of those who in different capacities work in the elementary school—the principal, his colleagues, the individual teacher and the pupils—was also examined.

The opportunity was also taken to assess the factors which inhibited the achievement of the aims of teaching by adapting from a previous study a schedule of 25 constraints, ranging from physical ones such as size and design of classrooms to such interpersonal ones as co-operation among staffs of schools, and including the possible constraint of student attitudes to learning and their home backgrounds (Taylor *et al.*, 1974).

Methodology and Scope
The main instrument of the study was a questionnaire, the first section of which asked for professional data on the teachers—length of teaching experience, grade taught, form of pupil grouping practiced, involvement in team teaching—and for certain personal data. The second section asked the teachers to rate, using a five-point scale, seven commonly ascribed general aims of elementary education such as 'the child's spiritual development', 'the child's emotional development' and 'the child's intellectual development' for the degree of emphasis which they would place on them in their teaching.

The third section embodied the 28 influences, and the teachers were asked to rate each for its degree of influence on '. . . what is taught in my school in general and on what is taught in my classroom in particular', and to give their rating on a five-point scale under two columns: one for 'School' and one for 'Classroom'. In addition they were asked to indicate whether or not they could reciprocate the influence by placing an 'R' alongside any influence which they could reciprocate.

A fourth section dealt with the 25 constraints. Here teachers were asked to indicate those constraints which they believed made for real difficulty in achieving their aims. A final section asked them to indicate their perception of the role of the teacher by selecting from four role descriptions, ranging from extremely child-centred to extremely teacher-dominant, the one which most closely approximated to their view of their role.

All 12 elementary schools in a moderately sized stable community in the Middle-west co-operated in the study and 73·3 per cent of its teachers completed the questionnaire.

Independent data were provided on certain relevant ecological characteristics of the schools—on the social class of its neighbourhood, the adequacy of the school's facilities, of staffing and of home-school relationship as well as the 'progressiveness' or otherwise of its educational programme.

Of the 136 teachers who responded, only two were men, 11 were single and only 31 had taught in their present school for more than five years. More than half had taught for less than six years and most (92) practised mixed ability grouping in their classrooms. All grade levels were about equally represented, and 49 of the teachers were involved in some form of team teaching.

The role modality of the teachers was distinctly 'teacher-centred'. All the responses were accorded (76 : 60) to the two essentially teacher-centred role descriptions, though it may be urged that the first of these ('the teacher guides, helps and encourages the child to do those things the child wishes to do, and to do certain things that the teacher considers desirable for the child to do') incorporates a degree of child-centredness. Even so, the strong tendency to be read from the teachers' responses is that of a predisposition toward teacher dominance, and a marked distance from the role ascription appropriate to 'child centred' education, at least in the British sense (Plowden, 1967).

In addition to a teacher-centred role modality, an emphasis on the aims of intellectual, social, emotional and moral development was found (Table 1). Spiritual development, as one would expect in a non-secular, state education system and in a society where religion is not only very much a personal matter but where it has also lost some of its hold over the minds of the people, was the least emphasized. Aesthetic and physical development took up a position of intermediate emphasis.

Table 1: Emphasis on aims

	\multicolumn{6}{c}{Rating}			
	1	2	3	4	5	0*	N	M	SD
Spiritual development	1	40	22	12	9	1	136	2.16	1.22
Aesthetic development	2	9	57	51	17	1	136	3.54	0.82
Physical development	0	9	45	63	17	0	136	3.62	0.84
Emotional development	0	1	11	50	74	0	136	4.45	0.67
Moral development	0	3	24	58	51	0	136	4.15	0.78
Social development	0	0	7	55	74	0	136	4.99	0.59
Intellectual development	0	0	3	35	98	0	136	4.70	0.50

* 0 = nil response.

The primacy of social and intellectual development as aims in elementary education is not at all surprising. The role of the elementary school in the development of nationhood is well documented (Cremin, 1965; Thayer and Levit, 1969). It is in the fostering of social mores and conventions that this has been achieved, but not at the expense of one of the prime purposes of schooling, the development of the intellect (Dreeben, 1970).

Though social and intellectual aims have primacy, none of the aims is markedly de-emphasised (i.e. rated 1). All are the concern of the teachers, though, as will be shown later, not equally for all grades or ages of teacher. Taken together, these aims represent a formidable array of purposes to be achieved and give to the elementary school teacher a broad and possibly diffuse role, one which is common to elementary school teachers elsewhere (Musgrove and Taylor, 1969).

In summary, these preliminary data suggest an almost entirely married female teaching force whose members have spent little time in their present schools, and in general no great length of time in the teaching profession; and which holds as important the aims of social and intellectual development, and transacts them in learning environments which are markedly teacher-centred. It is in relation to such a teaching force that the influences to which it is subjected (and which it exercises) as well as the constraints that set limits to its achievement will now be explored.

The Power to Influence
The power to influence what the elementary school teaches and what is taught in its classroom is not the prerogative of any one individual or group. The creation of state-wide elementary school systems in the development of American democracy ensured this. But some individuals and some groups exercise more influence than others. Which they are and what form of influence they exercise are matters to which we now turn.

It will be recalled that the teachers were asked to rate the degree of influence of 28 selected individuals, institutions and groups separately for 'influence on what is taught in my school' and 'what is taught in my classroom'. Table 2 sets out the data on the ratings of influences in general terms, and shows that if influence resides anywhere in the perceptions of the teachers it lies locally rather than nationally; and, pupils apart, in professional rather than in lay or community hands. Parents, for example, have an influence only at the margins of 'a definite influence' and the US Office of Education possesses 'only little influence'.

The strongest influences are seen to be those of the principal on what the school teaches, and the teachers on what is taught in its classrooms. Each occupies a dominant position in separate contexts of influence, with the principal sharing his influence with more extra-

Table 2: Degrees of influence: teachers' ratings

Item	SCHOOL *Description*	*Degree of Influence*
10	Principal of your school	Strong
	————————————4·0————————————	
2	Colleagues in your school	
6	Supervisory personnel	Definite to strong
16	Local Superintendent of schools	
	————————————3·5————————————	
12	Pupils in your school	
22	The School Board	
27	Occasional meetings of teachers	
7	Informal group of staff	
17	In-service training programmes	Definite
19	Formal staff meeting	
14	Yourself	
3	Local colleges and university	
11	Parents of children in your school	
	————————————3·0————————————	
26	Professional visitor to the school	
20	Textbook publishing company	
28	Colleagues in other schools	
1	Professional journals and papers	Little to definite
8	State Superintendent	
15	Educational writers and lecturers	
9	Press, radio, TV and other mass media	
	————————————2·5————————————	
18	Educational researcher	
4	Assistant principal*	
21	US Office of Education	Only little
25	Congress	
	————————————2·0————————————	
23	National Association of Education	
13	National reports	Little or none
5	Ford Foundation, etc.	
	————————————1·5————————————	
24	Church of any denomination	None

* Several of the schools did not have Assistant Principals.

school influences—Supervisory Personnel and the Local Superintendent—than the teachers. For the teachers, their pupils are seen to exercise a more potent influence than the local agents of educational administration.

Pupils would seem to exercise rather more influence, not only on what the school teaches but also on what is taught in its classrooms, than their age and status would seem to warrant. It may, of course, be argued that, as the *de facto* clients of the school, the exercise of such influence is to be expected. But what of the other clients of the school, their parents and the community? Their influence, as has already been noted, is only at the margins of 'a definite influence'. That they are

Table 2 continued

Item	CLASSROOM Description	Degree of Influence
14	Yourself	Strong
	————————————4·0————————————	
12	Pupils in your school	Definite to strong
10	Principal of your school	
	————————————3·5————————————	
2	Colleagues in your school	
6	Supervisory personnel	
27	Occasional meetings of teachers	Definite
17	In-service training programmes	
7	Informal group of staff	
19	Formal staff meeting	
	————————————3·0————————————	
11	Parents of children in your school	
3	Local colleges and university	
16	Local superintendent of schools	
22	The School Board	
28	Colleagues in other schools	Little to definite
1	Professional journals and papers	
26	Professional visitor to the school	
15	Educational writers and lecturers	
20	Textbook publishing company	
	————————————2·5————————————	
9	Press, radio, TV and other mass media	
18	Educational researcher	
4	Assistant principal*	Only little
8	State Superintendent	
25	Congress	
	————————————2·0————————————	
21	US Office of Education	
23	National Association of Education	Little or none
13	National reports	
5	Ford Foundation, etc.	
	————————————1·5————————————	
24	Church of any denomination	None

* Several of the schools did not have Assistant Principals.

represented in the School Board, which at least has a very definite influence on what the school teaches (though significantly less on what is taught in its classrooms), may be no more to parents and the community at large than a small consolation, leaving each with a feeling of powerlessness to influence how the minds and attitudes of children are shaped and their behaviour controlled.

Principals and teachers, formal and informal collegial groups, supervisory personnel and local agents of administration combine to provide the significant influences on the school and the classroom, though they share their influence with those for whom they cater—the pupils; those 'conscripted beneficiaries of the school system' (Dreeben, 1970).

Neither principal nor teacher share their influence over much with state or national agencies, nor with educational researchers—not even with the NEA, one of the largest professional teacher organizations in the world. And the mass media so potently influential in other spheres of national life, would appear to leave the teaching of the elementary school but little influenced. This insulation from wider societal influences is matched by the teachers' relative isolation from the influence of 'colleagues in other schools' who have only a negligible influence.

Local (if not parochial) and autonomous (if not self-regarding) in what teaching is done, the elementary school may also be an arena of conflict over what it teaches and is taught in its classrooms. Table 3 shows that there are significant differences among eight 'strong' to 'definite' influences. These differences may well serve to mark the boundary between school and classroom, between the influence of principals and that of the teachers, on the operational curriculum.

Table 3: Differences between means: school and classroom

		d	t	P
2	Colleagues in your school	+0·287	+3·23	·01
3	Local colleges and universities	+0·232	+2·09	·01
5	Ford Foundation, etc.	+0·198	+2·16	·05
6	Supervisory personnel	+0·265	+2·45	·05
8	State superintendent	+0·434	+3·76	·01
9	Principal of your school	+0·346	+2·79	·01
12	Pupils in your school	−0·309	−2·73	·01
14	Yourself	−1·331	−12·17	·01
16	Local superintendent	+0·574	+4·53	·01
22	School Board	+0·500	+4·30	·01
23	National Education Association	+0·228	+2·64	·01
25	Congress	+0·217	+1·79	·05

Colleagues, supervisory personnel, the School Board and the Local and State Superintendents of Schools, together with local colleges and the university, influence significantly more strongly what is taught by the school, over which the principal's influence is seen to be dominant, than what is taught in classrooms. Here the significantly stronger influences are seen to be those of the individual teacher—whose influence rises dramatically as the locus shifts from school to classroom —and the school's pupils. The influence of the individual teacher over what is taught in the classroom is considerably stronger than that of the principal over what is taught in the school, and is very largely exercised independently of the teacher's colleagues whose influence, in which the individual teacher participates, is exercised in greater measure over what the school teaches than on the teaching which goes on in individual classrooms. The degree of demarcation, if this term is appropriate, between school and classroom is underlined in the three remaining significant differences. Where influence is generally weak, the influence on the classroom is even weaker.

The evidence suggests a strong degree of autonomy for the classroom teacher: an autonomy which is exercised in relation to the pupils who are taught, though not without regard to the views of the principal whose influence on the classroom remains a definite one.

Reciprocation

Teachers, as Diagram 1 indicates, feel able in some degree to reciprocate all the influences to which they are subjected. But their ability to reciprocate the influence of the agents of local policy-making and administration—the School Board and the Local Superintendent of Schools—is not felt by them to be high. Like local colleges and the University, they are 'remote'. Even more remote, though understandably so, are the State and national agents of education.

Diagram 1: Representation of degrees of reciprocation

```
            100%─────────────────────────────────────────────
  High                          *Parents
                 *Colleagues    *Pupils
             75%─────────────────────────────────────────────
                 *Occasional    *Principal
                 meetings of
                 teachers
                                *Informal        *Colleagues in
                                Staff Group      other schools
DEGREE OF        *Supervisory
RECIPROCATION    Personnel
                      *In-service courses
                 *Formal staff meeting
             50%─────────────────────────────────────────────
                      *Professional visitors
                 *School
                 Board          *Local Superintendent
                 *Local Colleges
             25%─────────────────────────────────────────────
                      *Textbook Co.
                 *Professional        *Press, radio, TV
                 Journals        *Educational Researcher
                                      *Educational writers
   Low           *Ford Foundation etc.      *NEA Congress
                 *US Office of        *State Superintendent
                 Education       *Church
                 *National reports
              0%─────────────────────────────────────────────
```

M

Reciprocation with parents, pupils and colleagues, including the principal, is at a good level, as it is with Supervisory Personnel. It is perhaps not so satisfactory in Formal Staff Meetings, which in some cases may be designed to limit the degree of interaction by its formal rules and control of who has the 'right' to speak.

In general, the picture and pattern of reciprocation suggest a healthy interplay of influences and is in this respect superior to that found in other studies (Taylor, Reid, *et al.*, 1973). This indicates that the elementary school teacher is no mere functionary, unable to reciprocate in some degree the majority of influences to which she is subjected. Rather, she belongs to a system which appears to be participatory, open to the reciprocation by her of those influences.

Structure of Influence

Influence is not simply of one kind. It takes many forms. What are these as they are exercised on what the elementary school teaches and on what is taught in its classrooms ? An answer can be attempted using the ratings of the teachers for influences on both school and classroom. The statistical technique used is a common though complex one, that of Factor Analysis. At its simplest, it sorts the influences into the groups to which they belong, sometimes putting them into more than one group if they exercise more than one kind of influence. For example, the principal acts on some occasions as the formal head of an institution and on others as an 'expert' on educational matters. His influence is, thus, by turns 'administrative or bureaucratic', in that it arises from the office he holds, and on others it is the influence of 'expertise', arising from the knowledge he has acquired from his experience and study of education. Each kind of influence is distinct.

The ratings for influence, when analysed, produced five reliable groupings. (See Appendix 1 for full details.) Each is described below, in order of its size, paying particular attention to the four or five influences which help to define the form of the influence which is exercised.

School based client and issues focussed influence (Factor 5)
The three highest loadings, i.e. those carrying most weight, in this group were the influence of the principal and the mass media (press, radio and TV) on the school and the formal staff meeting on the class-room. In addition the influences of parents, supervisory personnel, colleagues, the informal group of staff, local colleges, educational researchers and writers together with the local and state superintendent

of schools, and the School Board are to be found in this group. More than half the specific influences appear for both influence on the school and the classroom.

With the strong definition of the influence of the principal on the school, the presence of the formal staff meetings, of colleagues, and informal groups of staff together with parents and the agencies of supervision and administration there would appear to be a grouping of influences much concerned with the functioning of the school as an institution. Its head (the principal), its clients (the parents), its work force (the teachers), together with its agents of control (supervisory and administrative personnel) and its political master (the School Board), have a common cause in the issues which confront the school—issues concerned with what should be taught, for what purpose and in what way. An issue is raised by the media, by educational writers and researchers and the principal may be called on to declare a point of view on it, to look to his staff for support and to persuade parents of its validity. He may have to be prepared for difficulties with the administration and for the *issue*, a matter of contention and controversy, to reach the agenda of a meeting of the School Board. Sex education, discipline, interpersonal and race relations are but some of the educational issues to which the elementary school has had to respond in recent years.

It is the dominant presence of both the formal head of the school and the mass media which give this grouping of influences its particular quality: *the school* makes a response to issues raised, acknowledging as it does so the need for staff support, for parental approval and at least the concurrence of the administration and the acquiescence of those politically responsible for the school. It is for these reaons that this sub-system of influences is described as school-based, and client- and issues-focused.

In all probability the influence represented here is, as has been suggested, political in form, seeking to maintain an equilibrium among those with interests in the activities of the school and to discharge those demands placed on the school which have become controversial in ways acceptable to all concerned. As Dreeben (1970) points out:

'Wherever political control rests, school systems are subjected to multiple pressures reflecting the interests of diverse groups in the community, and they vary in their vulnerability to them.' (page 43).

This sub-system of influence shows the wide range of pressures that the curriculum of the school may have to accommodate. Earlier data

(p. 174–5) suggest that it is those who work within the school—the principal and his staff—who will have most influence on the decisions about the way in which what the school teaches is shaped to meet these pressures. In some cases more will be done in the appearance than in the reality. Great shifts and striving in curriculum change will be seen but the outcome may leave the schools and their curricula much as before: in fact, as the principal and his staff consider it ought to be (Erlach, 1972). Nevertheless, issues will have been defused to the satisfaction of all concerned, at least in the short term.

Teacher professional classroom based influence (Factor 2)
Just as the school as an institution focusses on itself a structure of influences, so does the individual teacher—not influences concerned with issues, but collegial, professional influences. Meetings of teachers, colleagues both in their own and other schools, the teacher herself and professional journals group together to form this sub-system of influences and find in students and in in-service programmes additional support. Classroom influences tend to be more marked than school influences and on the whole there is a preoccupation with the teacher's personal professional concerns. There is no evidence here of the influence of the principal, the administration or parents. There are only professional influences and those of the profession's immediate clients, the students. The influences are not simply personal, merely the concerns of practitioners, they also include the values conveyed by professional journals and through in-service programmes. The major influence of values is in fact to be found in the next sub-system of influences.

Educational values: ideological influence (Factor 3)
What is educational is a matter of deciding what is both proper and worthwhile to teach the young and it is not surprising to find one group of influences devoted to the generalized influence of educational values. The church, symbolizing as it does moral forces, together with local colleges and university, defines educational values with the support of educational researchers, the work of such philanthropic social agencies as the Ford Foundation, the pronouncements of the NEA and findings like those of the Coleman Report. The values implicit in the workings of government and the political system (suggested in this particular grouping by the presence of Congress) are influential also. In addition, the presence of the mass media serves to suggest the many-sided, and sometimes controversial nature of educational values. However, there

is a sense in which prevailing educational values take on the qualities of an ideology in that they accept certain value positions having good currency in society (Schon, 1972) as axiomatic—to be taken on trust, beyond controversy, or as a matter of belief. It is this characteristic which makes this sub-system of influences an *ideological* one.

Advisory or expert influence (Factor 4)
Expertise about what to teach in elementary schools comes from many sources. These sources, collectively, constitute the *advisory* or *expert* sub-system of influences—textbooks, in their content; educational researchers, in their reports; principals, superintendents of schools, educational writers, because of their experience and knowledge; the Office of Education, by its recommendations; reports of surveys, supervisory personnel, in their suggestions; and in-service programmes—can all offer some form of advice about what the elementary school teaches. Pupils, also, in their response to what is taught, by their interest and involvement, become in a sense the data of expertise and it is not surprising to find them in this group of influences.

Administrative and bureaucratic influence (Factor 1)
From Congress to the School Board and from the Office of Education to the State Superintendent (all of which are found in this group) flows the *administration* of education which influences what schools teach by the provision of staff, materials and resources. It also lays down the ground rules within which schools are to operate; rules which parents and even pupils will from time to time insist are kept. The influence of administration, its ordering of appropriate ways for doing things, and for securing the necessary staff and materials, can be powerfully inhibiting or facilitating of what the school teaches—largely, but not solely, by its control of resources. Its control of rights, those of parents and pupils, for example, also was an influence. Bureaucracy, therefore, has its power to influence the curriculum and, with administrative influence, makes up the last of the five sub-systems of influences.

The Curricular Influence System
That the operational curriculum of the elementary school should be open to influence is only to be expected, and the five sub-systems described above suggest the kinds of influence to which it is subjected. Each sub-system exercises its influence in a distinctive way and may well call for a different response on the part of teachers. For example, the classroom-based professional influence of teachers may be exercised

through a call to teachers to subscribe to professional norms, to do in the classroom what the profession considers ought to be done, and to stand on their professional dignity if their authority to make classroom-based decisions is challenged. School-based influence calls for a different response, one which will lead to the creation of a policy toward any issue to which the school, both as an institution and as a group of people with formal responsibility, needs to respond. The issue has to be taken on board, examined and, if it cannot be rejected, rendered harmless so that parents, the public and the administration feel it 'safe' to leave the matter in the hands of the school.

In these sorts of ways response is constructed through the sub-systems of influence which together form the environmental forces in relation to which what is taught by the school and in its classrooms is shaped and fashioned, day by day, by those individuals, organizations and institutions with an interest in what is taught to the young children of elementary school age. Diagram 2 represents the interlocking of the separate sub-systems which make up the curricular influence system of the elementary school.

Constraints on Teaching

Elsewhere it has been said:

> 'Constraints inhibit and circumscribe the extent to which an ideal state of affairs can be achieved. They set limits to our best efforts whatever the setting, whether it is public or private. In the (elementary) school the lack of facilities, of equipment, books and aterials, them teacher's level of competence, training or readiness to co-operate with (her) colleagues; the rigidity of the (daily schedule), the style of discipline employed and the number of children in a class are each likely to set limits to what the school can teach.' (Taylor *et al.*, 1974.)

What sets limits to the extent to which elementary school teachers can achieve the aims which they set themselves? What circumscribes what they can teach? It was to answer these and other related questions that the teachers were asked to indicate for each of 25 constraints those which 'make for real difficulty in achieving your aims'. Diagram 3 groups them under areas of constraint—Physical and Resource Constraints, Constraints of Children and their Homes, Policy and Institutional Constraints, and Staff Constraints—and suggests the degree to which they may be constraining on the achievement of teachers' curricular aims.

Diagram 2: *The interlock of the curricular influence sub-system of the elementary school*

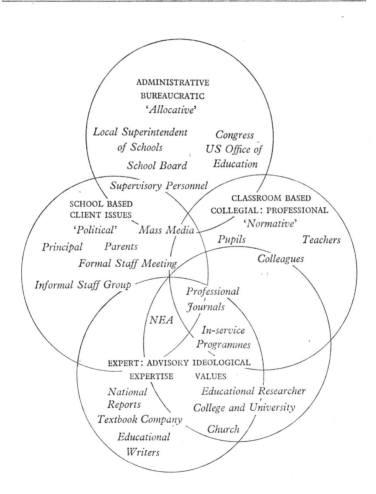

The most marked single constraint is 10. Children's home environment, and Constraints of Children—their abilities, attitudes, previous experience of being taught and the number in class—is the strongest group of constraints. This is followed by Physical and Resource Constraints where such constraints as sound insulation and air conditioning, and size of classrooms are seen as particularly constraining. Staff and Policy and Institutional Constraints, surprisingly enough, do not seem to be significant groups of constraints presenting real difficulties to the teachers. Although teachers are critical of their training, of state

Diagram 3: Percentage constraints by item and area

	PERCENTAGE CONSTRAINT 10 20 30 40 50 60	ADJUSTED MEANS %
Physical and *Resource* *Constraints*	15. Physical conditions 20. Provision of Teachers Aides 22. Teaching Materials 23. Size of classrooms 24. Specialist facilities	24·0
Constraints *of Children* *and Home*	6. Number of children in class 7. Abilities of children 10. Children's home environment 14. Age of children 16. Attitudes of children 21. Children's previous experience	33·3
Policy and *Institutional* *Constraints*	1. School regulations 2. Range of school activities 3. Class organization 11. Liaison between schools 13. Daily schedule 17. Quality of communication 12. State educational policy	9·5
Staff *Constraints*	3. Level of professional training 4. Co-operation between staff 5. Time off to attend courses 9. Readiness of staff 18. In-service training 19. Level of competence 25. Changes in staff	9·9
	Constraints | *Significant* *Constraints* | *Strong* *Constraints* | *Very Strong* *Constraints*	

educational policies and of school regulations, most do not see them standing in the way of what they wish to achieve through their teaching.

An analysis to group the constraints (see Appendix 2) suggests six areas rather than the four employed so far. Three coincided: Constraints of Children, of Staff and Physical and Resource Constraints which included such 'services' as the provision of in-service education for teachers.

Internal Classroom Constraints—size and design of classroom, number of children in class, form of daily schedule and physical conditions—were grouped together, as were liaison between schools, changes in staff, provision of aides, etc. into an area of External School Constraints, that is constraints arising from the environment in which the school is set.

The final group of the six can only be very tentatively defined. It included quality of communication about what should be taught, the form of State educational policy, children's previous experience of being taught and their home environment, as well as the form of daily schedule. Such a grouping would seem to suggest External Classroom Constraints, that is, constraints which impinge on the classroom either from within the school or from the general social environment.

Such groupings, tentative though some may be, do suggest one or two broad dimensions along which to locate constraints and headings under which to describe them. The dimension Internal/External would seem useful, as do the descriptions of Resources, Staff or Task-group and Classroom though this last could be described as 'technological constraints on teaching'. Constraints of Children does, however, present a problem: are they internal or external constraints? Children are the raw material on which teachers must work. They are an 'input' from outside, external to the school and classroom. Without them there would be no aims to be achieved or to be frustrated. They also represent the achievement of the teacher's aims in their developed skills and capabilities, and in this respect are an 'output' of teaching and 'internal' to the school and the classroom. Their dual nature as both 'external' and 'internal' constraints, as both the input to and the output of the teaching process makes teaching an especially complex task. It is in no way remarkable, therefore, that children should be a major source of constraints on the achievement of the aims of teaching. They have been defined as the 'throughput' of the institution (Herriott and Hodgkins, 1973). But they may be more than this.

Waller (1932), in his classic *The Sociology of Teaching*, pointed out yet a further way in which students may constrain teaching. Not only are 'pupils the material in which teachers are supposed to produce results but, pupils are human beings trying to realize themselves—striving to produce their own results in their own way.' (page 196)

The students' attempts to realize themselves suggest that they are not simply an institution's throughput but a positive force acting on and reacting to the school's treatment of them.

Making Connections

Not all teachers emphasized equally the same aims, nor gave to specific influences or constraints the same weight. Table 4 shows the differences which were significant and the teaching group to which they relate. Not all can be readily explained.

That Kindergarten and Grade 1 teachers should see a marked influence on the school of local colleges and the university is not the least surprising. In the school system concerned, the University in particular has vigorously pioneered advanced methods for teaching very young children. Nor is it surprising that these teachers see the provision of teaching aides (or the lack of them) and children's home background as constraints. Dealing with groups of very young children calls for ancillary help, and the success with which the young child can be helped to adjust to the school depends very much on the homes from which they come.

For inexperienced teachers what college or university taught them still counts for something, and so does the local superintendent, possibly because their future in the profession may depend on his approval and evaluation. Long-serving teachers find the number of children in a class more constraining than less experienced teachers, though why this should be so is difficult to explain. It may be a function of their age or of their awareness that the objectives of teaching in the elementary school have grown in both scale and scope in recent decades to such an extent that a teacher can only hope to achieve them with fewer children to teach.

The influence of the formal staff meeting on the school, the principal and professional visitors on the classroom and the constraints of the size and design of the classroom were seen by the teachers involved in team teaching as stronger influences and constraints than they were seen by teachers who were not involved in team teaching.

That the size and design of classrooms should be seen by these teachers as a more marked constraint is understandable. Team teaching calls at one time for large group teaching and at others for individualized instruction as well as the many sizes of group in between. The conventional classroom hardly provides the flexibility necessary for such a range of teaching–learning groups. Its very design must at times frustrate the aims of teachers engaged in team teaching.

But why team-teachers should see the influence of the principal and the professional visitor on their teaching, and that of the formal staff meeting on what the school teaches, as stronger is not so readily explained. Team teaching, as several writers have pointed out, makes teachers more visible, and therefore more open to the influence of others through the evaluations which are made of their teaching performance. The evidence on this score is convincing (Marran, Dornbusch and Scott, 1972). This may be why the principal and professional visitors are seen as stronger influences: because team teaching has greater visibility. But visibility does not explain the greater influence of the formal staff meeting. Here the role might be that of legitimizing and approving a teaching policy and monitoring its implementation and success in those schools where team teaching is employed. However, a close study of such schools would be needed to validate this suggestion.

Just as the adoption of an innovative mode of teaching appears to give rise to somewhat different strengths of influence and constraint, so does an innovative style of grouping students for learning. In this case in mixed ability groups, Table 2 shows that two influences on the school—professional visitors and Congress—and one on the classroom—pupils—take on an enhanced potency, and two constraints—of children's attitudes and home environment—are seen as more marked.

Mixed ability grouping in the elementary schools is partly a practical response to the call for equality of educational opportunity, and this may be why Congress is seen as having a greater influence on what the school teaches in those schools where mixed ability grouping is practised; and partly a response to the adverse psychological consequences for the child which may arise under forms of learning which depend on discrimination based on ability levels. It is in this way that the greater influence of professional visitors may be explained.

In practice, success in the teaching of a mixed ability group will depend on the readiness of the children to adapt to individualized learning programmes and their capacity for self-programming and self-motivation (Westbury, 1973). The individual child—his behaviour and attitudes—is thus a crucial variable in the mixed ability classroom, hence his greater influence on what is taught, and the greater the constraint of his attitudes and home environment on the achievement of desirable outcomes (Resnick, 1972).

Table 4: Relationships between variables

INDEPENDENT VARIABLE	DIRECTION OF EMPHASIS OR INFLUENCE, ETC.	AIM, INFLUENCE OR CONSTRAINT	P
Teaching Group			
Kindergarten and Grade 1	Greater emphasis	Physical development	·01
Kindergarten and Grade 1	Greater influence on school	Local colleges and university	·05
Kindergarten and Grade 1	Greater constraint	Children's home environment	·05
Kindergarten and Grade 1	Greater constraint	Provision of aides	·01
Length Teaching Experience			
Teachers with 5 years or less	Greater emphasis	Emotional development	·05
Teachers with 5 years or less	Greater influence on school	Local colleges and university	·01
Teachers with 5 years or less	Greater influence on classroom	Local Superintendent	·05
Teachers with more than 5 years	Greater constraint	Number of children	·05
Teachers with 5 years or less	Greater constraint	Physical conditions	·05
Length Time in Present School			
Teachers with 5 years or less	Greater emphasis	Physical development	·05
Teachers with 5 years or less	Greater emphasis	Intellectual development	·05
Teachers with more than 5 years	Greater constraint	Daily schedule	·01
Team Teaching			
Teachers involved in team teaching	Greater influence on school	Formal staff meeting	·05
Teachers involved in team teaching	Greater influence on classroom	Principal	·05
Teachers involved in team teaching	Greater influence on classroom	Professional visitors	·01
Teachers involved in team teaching	Great constraint	Size and design of classroom	·01
Form of Grouping			
Teachers involved in mixed ability grouping	Greater influence on school	Professional visitors	·05
Teachers involved in mixed ability grouping	Greater influence on school	Congress	·05
Teachers involved in mixed ability grouping	Greater influence on classroom	Pupils	·05
Teachers involved in mixed ability grouping	Greater constraint	Children's home environment	·05
Teachers involved in mixed ability grouping	Greater constraint	Children's attitudes	·01

Lastly in this section are those teachers with less than five years' teaching in their present schools, a majority of the teachers sampled, who tend to emphasize the aims of physical and intellectual development to a greater extent than their colleagues who have served longer in the schools. This latter group of teachers also see the form of the daily schedule as more constraining. Why these differences arise is not easy to explain. More detailed case studies would be needed before a reliable explanation would become possible.

Consensus and the Ecology of the Schools

How far are the teachers within a school agreed on the aims which guide their teaching and what are the correlates of different levels of agreement if such exist? This is the question now explored.

It was clear from Table 1 (p. 172), which gave the level of emphasis which teachers in general place on aims, that a good level of agreement was likely to be found between teachers in particular schools. This in fact turned out to be the case (see Table 5). Most of the measures of consensus are significant at a very high level. However, though there is a high level agreement among staffs of schools on the aims to be emphasized, especially those of social and intellectual development, the level of consensus is higher in some schools than in others.

Table 5: Degree of consensus on aims

School No.	Coefficient of Concordance*	Sig. Level
1	0·61	·001
2	0·56	·001
3	0·69	·001
4	0·49	·001
5	0·62	NS**
6	0·69	·001
7	0·73	·001
8	0·56	·001
9	0·50	·001
10	0·71	·001
11	0·55	·001
12	0·53	·005

* Kendal's coefficient of concordance was considered to be the most suitable measure of consensus.

** This school provided only a small sample of teachers and was omitted from subsequent analysis.

These differing levels of consensus were related to certain independent variables—length of teaching experience and length of time in present school, to the perceived influence of the principal, the formal staff meeting and the textbook company, as well as to the constraints of the children's home background and provision of teachers' aides. In addition, the progressiveness of the curriculum was related to the levels of consensus. Table 6 shows the direction of the relationships.

Table 6: Correlates of consensus on aims within schools

Variable	Consensus	Level Sig.
Length of teaching	High	·01
Time in present school	High	·01
Influences		
Principal on School	High	·05
Principal on Classroom	High	·05
Formal Staff Meeting on School	High	·05
Formal Staff Meeting on Classroom	High	·05
Textbook Company on School	High	·05
Textbook Company on Classroom	High	·05
Constraints		
Children's Home Background	High	·001
Provision of Teacher's Aides	High	·01
Ecological Factors		
Progressiveness of Curriculum	High	·001

The correlates of a very high agreement on aims are not without interest. A principal who makes his presence felt both at school and classroom levels may well induce teachers to emphasize a common set of aims. Similarly, where the formal staff meeting has strong influence, teachers may agree to emphasize a particular set of aims. Teachers may also be in considerable agreement on aims where much of what the school teaches and is taught in its classrooms is determined by the textbooks used.

Constraints too, not surprisingly, relate to levels of consensus concerning aims. In schools where the home background is seen as a marked constraint, teachers share a high agreement on aims. Whether this is merely the constraint of a 'poor' home is not evident in the data, though with children from somewhat disadvantaged backgrounds teachers may feel that they ought to concentrate their teaching on 'what matters'. It could also be that the press of expectations for 'results' in academic terms, for reading and writing, of the parents of children from middle-class backgrounds also induces a high consensus on aims. Only further study can set the record right.

Similarly with teachers' aides, why is their absence related to a high consensus on aims? The data suggest that this is so but fail to supply sufficient additional information to allow of a satisfactory explanation.

The relationship of high consensus and progressiveness of the curriculum is much easier to explain. The relationship is positive. The more progressive the curriculum of a school, the higher was the level of consensus. Here we have an instance of the commitment of staff to a mode of teaching and learning which is a departure from the ordinary and conventional. It is a commitment which provides a 'common cause' and such, no doubt, is expressed in a high level of agreement on the aims to be emphasized.

With such generally high levels of agreement on aims as this study has shown to exist, it seemed unlikely that a study of the factor related to levels of consensus would be very productive, and this has turned out to be so, though some light has been cast on aspects of the role of the principal and of the formal staff meeting, as well as on the progressiveness of the school curriculum. However, rather more detail is needed than was attained in this study if the determinants of consensus are to be put beyond doubt.

Overview
Lortie (1969) commented in the preliminaries to his essay on elementary school teaching that, in occupations where members claim a professional status and claim membership of a specialized group of colleagues, '... the several strands of hierarchical control, collegial control and autonomy become tangled and complex'. Whether what was claimed to be the consequence for the control exercised by a certain group of people is correct or not, it would certainly seem to be true for control of the curriculum. Here the complexity resides in the separation of influence over what the school teaches and what is taught in its classrooms. The separation is essentially of the influence of the principal, bound as he is by the checks and balances of parents, the local administration, the school board and by the staff meeting, and that of the teachers whose influence on what is taught in the classroom is paramount. The teacher's influence is, however, moderated by that which the children whom she teaches can bring to bear through their response to the kind of teaching in which the teacher considers it her professional duty to engage.

This separation or zoning of influence over what is taught within the elementary school would seem to be very real indeed, given the way in which the teachers define their situation. Their definition of the situation is their reality and (Thomas, 1928; McHugh, 1968) this reality, as a consequence, becomes for those individuals and institutions with a legitimate concern for what the elementary school teaches *the* reality with which they must treat, over which they must manage transactions, make changes and deal with issues of ideology and of values. It is not, therefore, at all surprising that the school board, the local and state superintendents of schools, parents and the Office of Education may become all too quickly enmeshed in a confusion of spheres of influence, of powers, of interests, priorities, beliefs and rights in their dealing with the elementary school and its teachers. Nor is it surprising that teachers for their part frequently feel that the 'administration' has its agenda wrong, that it is the reality of the classroom, its demands for supervision and control, which should be of first concern. And their strictures may be as frequently directed at principals for their preoccupation with the anxieties of parents as at the administrators who govern the resources of schools.

There can be little doubt that the strength of influence which the teacher possesses to determine what is taught in her classroom, is not hers by right as would be the case in more highly developed professions but is *de facto* an influence which she sees herself both possessing and exercising. Though not in the strict sense an honest woman, she is in the strict sense a powerful one though not to the extent of exercising her power in an entirely arbitrary way. Her exercise of influence is not wholly autonomous. It is tempered by her membership of a collegial group and in terms of her beliefs about how her colleagues would exercise their influence in the same situation. And the focus for the exercise of influence are the core transactions of teaching; her relationships with her students; and (transactions which are at the heart of her autonomy) the free exercise of decisions about what to teach and how to teach it. It is here that as Lortie has it, 'she shifts and sorts various ideas before applying them in ways she regards as effective' (*op. cit.*).

Of course the teacher's autonomy is not unchallenged. Her constraints are not, in the main, of competence, of training or of relationships with colleagues nor of the policies and procedures through which schools are managed, but are mainly physical (especially those on the classroom) and constraints attaching to children—the number to be taught, their abilities and attitudes and their home background. It is from those at the heart of daily transactions—the children to be taught —that most constraints arise, just as it is the children who exert considerable influence not only on what is taught in the classroom but also on what the school teaches.

In their twin capacity to be influential and to bring to bear severe constraints, the very presence of children in the elementary school may account considerably for the zoning of influence, the need and press for autonomy by the teacher, and the weak leverage on the school system which both the public and the administration possess. But the locus of influence and constraint may also be of considerable importance. The conventional classroom with the meaning which it imposes on teaching may well be the crucial factor in generating patterns of curricular influence (Westbury, 1973).

The conventional classroom, at least in terms of the reality which it represents to teachers, is undergoing changes. Individualized, self-paced instruction employing structured materials, team teaching, mixed ability grouping and interest-based learning projects are but some of the current explorations which may give a new meaning to teaching. They could well create new alignments of influence (and most likely change the weighting of present constraints) and erode established boundaries. What would be gained from this and what lost it, is not possible to say with certainty but it would seem from the available evidence that there could be some loss of autonomy to the teacher and some gain to the influence of the principal and to the formal staff group. The *de facto* result might well be elementary schools run by boards of directors (the teachers) with an executive head (the principal). There is no evidence, however, to suggest that the administration or the public would gain, and the issue of who controls what it is proper to teach the young seems likely to remain one of conflict.

But conflict or no, it would seem from the evidence that it is the teacher in the classroom who *is* crucial in determining what *is* taught, and in giving it meaning. For her, reward and satisfaction currently lie 'where the action is', especially in relationships with her students. As Sarason (1971) has pointed out '. . . among all the aspects of the school culture that are or may be the objects of change, none is as important as the quality of life and thinking in the classroom. . . .' (p. 235). It is this quality of life that is the operational curriculum and at present it can be changed only by consent of the teachers and the acquiescence of the taught. In the future, however, it may be changed by changing the culture of learning as may be happening with team teaching and 'open' education. But even when changed it is more than likely, either through the mechanisms already available or through ones yet to be developed, that teachers will retain their influence on the curriculum and the principal his on the broad framework of what the school teaches. The reason for this is not far to seek. Neither teachers nor principals would have any meaningful identity without the considerable right, legitimate or otherwise, to influence what their students learn. It is perhaps in the direction of sharpening and completing identities, that solutions to the problems created by zones of influence may be resolved. It may be that teachers in particular have a greater contribution to make to the resolution of educational issues and to the form and style of administration, and advice to schools. It may also be that they carry too little responsibility because their authority is *de facto* rather than *de jure*, and an adjustment of this in the direction of a formal responsibility for what the school engages in and for the quality of life in its classrooms could result in legitimizing the influence which they now exert. It might also give teachers a stake in events beyond the walls of their own classrooms. Though such moves would enhance the authority and stature of teachers—something which some consider is long overdue—it would not diminish the contention over what it is proper to teach the young. Views on this derive from beliefs about life which differ fundamentally and relate to deep seated divisions in social attitudes (Douglas, 1973; Kerlinger, 1959).

References

CENTRAL ADVISORY COUNCIL (1967) *Plowden Report: Children and their Primary Schools*. London: HMSO.

CREMIN, L. A. (1965) *The Genius of American Education*. Pittsburgh University, Pittsburgh Press.

DREEBEN, R. (1970) *The Nature of Teaching*. Glenview, Ill.: Scott, Foreman and Co.

DOUGLAS, M. (1973) *Natural Symbols*. Harmondsworth: Penguin.

ERLACH, J. W. (1972) 'Curriculum development for urban education', *Urban Rev.*, 5, 5, 23–29.

HERRIOTT, R. E., and HODGKINS, B. J. (1973) *The Environment of Schooling*. New Jersey: Prentice Hall.

KERLINGER, F. N. (1967) 'The first and second-order factor structure of attitudes toward education', *Amer. Educ. Res. J.*, 4, 191–205.

LORTIE, D. C. (1969) 'The Balance of Control and Autonomy in Elementary School Teaching'. In Etzioni, A. (Ed.) *The Semi-Professions and their Organization*. New York: Free Press.

MARRAN, G. D., DORNBUSCH, S. M., and SCOTT, W. R. (1972) *The Professionalism of Elementary School Teachers*. Mimeo. Stanford University.

MCHUGH, P. S. (1968) *Defining the Situation*. New York: Bobbs-Merrill.

MUSGROVE, F., and TAYLOR, P. H. (1969) *Society and the Teacher's Role*. London: Routledge and Kegan Paul.

PARSONS, T. (1963) 'On the concept of influence', *Pub. Op. Qu.*, 27, 1, 37–62.

RESNICK, L. (1972) 'Teacher behaviour in the informal classroom', *J. Curric. Studies*, 4, 2, 99–109.

SARASON, S. B. (1971) *The Culture of the School and the Problem of Change*. Boston: Allyn and Bacon.

SCHON, D. A. (1970) *Beyond the Stable State*. London: Temple Smith.

TAYLOR, P. H., and REID, W. A. (1971) 'A study of the curricular influence system of the English primary school', *Scand. J. Educ. Res.*, 16, 1–23.

TAYLOR, P. H., REID, W. A., HOLLEY, B., and EXON, G. (1974) *Purpose Power and Constraint in the Primary School Curriculum*. London: Macmillan for the Schools Council.

TAYLOR, P. H., and ADAMS, R. S. (1974) 'Influences on the curriculum of teachers' colleges', *J. Curric. Studies*.

TAYLOR, P. H. (1974) 'Lecturers' perceptions of the influence of ideas on the curriculum of colleges of education', *Brit. J. Educ. Psychol.*, 44, 2, 131–139.

TAYLOR, P. H., REID, W. A., and HOLLEY, B. J. (1974) *The English Sixth Form*. London: Routledge and Kegan Paul.

THAYER, V. T., and LEVIT, M. (1969) *The Role of the School in American Society*. 2nd ed. New York: Dodd, Mead & Co.

THOMAS, W. I. (1928) *The Child in America*. New York: Knopf.

WALLER, W. (1932) *The Sociology of Teaching*. New York: John Wiley.

WESTBURY, L. (1973) 'Conventional classrooms, "open" classrooms and the technology of teaching', *J. Curric. Studies*, 5, 2.

Appendix 1

Factor Analysis of School and Classroom Influences

Factor 1

C51	Congress	724	
S24	Congress	695	
C48	The School Board	628	
C47	US Office of Education	626	
C49	National Associations of Education, e.g. NEA	602	
S20	Textbook publishing company	573	
S21	US Office of Education	545	
S22	The School Board	522	
C35	Press, radio and TV	513	
C34	State Superintendent of Schools	459	
S11	Pupils in your schools	409	
S7	State Superintendent of Schools	394	
C37	Parents of children in your school	392	
C38	Pupils in your school	366	
C42	Local superintendent of schools	360	
S8	Press, radio and TV	360	$V = 7 \cdot 21 \%$
S10	Parents of children in your school	318	

Factor 2

C53	Occasional meetings of teachers	723
S26	Occasional meetings of teachers	718
C54	Colleagues in other schools	614
S27	Colleagues in other schools	554
C40	Yourself	527
C29	Colleagues in your school	519
C28	Professional Journals	492

C38	Pupils in your school	489	
S11	Pupils in your school	445	
S25	Professional visitors	439	
S1	Professional journals	428	
C43	In-service training programmes	418	
S2	Colleagues in your school	401	
C16	In-service training programmes	367	
C52	Professional visitors	371	
S6	Supervisory personnel	364	$V = 10.44\%$
S13	Yourself	313	

Factor 3

C50	Church of any denomination	752	
S23	Church of any denomination	741	
S3	Local colleges and universities	639	
S4	Ford Foundation, etc.	639	
C31	Ford Foundation, etc.	593	
S17	Educational researchers	387	
S22	National Associations of Education, e.g. NEA	384	
S8	Press, radio, TV and other media	373	
S12	National Reports, e.g. Coleman Report	335	
C49	National Associations of Education	348	
S25	Congress	346	
C39	National Reports, e.g. Coleman Report	339	
C44	Educational Researchers	321	
C52	Professional visitors to the school	306	$V = 9.55\%$
C35	Press, radio, TV and other media	302	

Factor 4

C46	Textbook publishing company	632	
C44	Educational researchers	614	
S7	State Superintendent of Schools	613	
S10	Principal of your school	592	
S17	In-service training programmes	575	
C34	State Superintendent of Schools	569	
S20	Textbook publishing company	544	
C41	Educational writers and lecturers	540	
S15	Local Superintendent of Schools	509	
S12	Pupils in your school	505	
C47	US Office of Education	500	
C42	Local Superintendent of Schools	488	
C39	National Reports, e.g. Coleman Report	468	
S14	National Reports, e.g. Coleman Report	467	
S5	Supervisory personnel	424	
C32	Supervisory personnel	398	
C43	In-service training programmes	364	$V = 9.05\%$
S16	In-service training programmes	331	

Factor 5

C36	Principal of your school	801	
S9	Press, radio and TV	743	
C45	Formal staff meeting	604	
S18	Educational researcher	574	
C37	Parents	518	

S10	Principal of your school	509	
S6	Supervisory personnel	514	
C29	Colleagues in your school	496	
C33	Informal group of staff	490	
S3	Local colleges and universities	489	
S15	Educational writers and lecturers	483	
S5	Ford Foundation, etc.	457	
C42	Local Superintendent of Schools	445	
S2	Colleagues in your school	439	
S21	US Office of Education	417	
C30	Local colleges and universities	404	
C32	Supervisory personnel	389	
S8	State Superintendent of Schools	385	
C48	The School Board	323	$V=10.66\%$
C35	Press, radio and TV	311	
S16	Local Superintendent of Schools	304	

Appendix 2

Factor Analysis of Constraints

Factor 1

18	Level of provision of in-service education	821	
24	Provision of specialist facilities	688	
9	Readiness of staff	511	
22	Level of provision of teaching materials	476	
15	Physical conditions	464	
21	Children's previous experience	341	$V=9.68\%$

Factor 2

7	Abilities of children	784	
16	Attitudes of children	655	
10	Children's home environment	562	
14	Age of children	533	
8	Form of class organization	481	
2	Range of school activities	−318	$V=8.87\%$

Factor 3

11	Liaison between schools	762	
25	Changes in staff	660	
5	Time off to attend courses	474	
20	Provision of teacher's aides	302	
21	Children's previous experience	229	
15	Physical conditions	214	
8	Form of class organization	+340	$V=6.98\%$

Factor 4

23	Size and design of classrooms	663	
6	Number of children in class	608	

13	Form of daily schedule	588	
15	Physical conditions	344	
20	Provision of teacher's aides	375	
5	Time off to attend courses	300	
8	Form of class organization	291	
9	Readiness of staff	−288	$V=7.38\%$

Factor 5

17	Quality of communication	570	
12	Form of state educational policy	533	
21	Children's previous experience of being taught	456	
10	Children's home environment	322	
13	Form of daily schedule	302	
6	Number of children in class	−393	$V=6.40\%$

Factor 6

3	Level of professional training of teachers	633	
19	Your own level of competence	610	
4	Co-operation between teachers	593	
1	Style of school regulations	513	
22	Level of provision of teaching material	366	
25	Changes in staff	356	
2	Range of school activities	383	$V=8.63\%$

This study was made possible by the help of the staff of the Center for Research in Social Behaviour, University of Missouri, to whom grateful acknowledgements are made, and by a grant from the Social Science Research Council for a programme of studies in curriculum theory.